COBOL Reference Manual

MERANT, INC

Acknowledgements

This COBOL Reference Manual contains material based on ANS X3.23-1985, the American National Standard for COBOL. That publication requests that documents using material from it should contain the following acknowledgement.

COBOL is an industry language and is not the property of any company or group of companies, or of any organization or group of organizations.

No warranty, expressed or implied, is made by any contributor or by the CODASYL Programming Language Committee as to the accuracy and functioning of the programming system and language. Moreover, no responsibility is assumed by any contributor, or by the committee, in connection therewith.

The authors and copyright holders of the copyright material used herein:

FLOW-MATIC (trademark for Sperry Rand Corporation) Programming the Univac (R) I and II, Data Automation Systems copyrighted 1958, 1959, by Sperry Rand Corporation; IBM Commercial Translator Form No. F28-8013, copyrighted 1959 by IBM; FACT, DSI27 A5260-2760, copyrighted 1960 by Minneapolis-Honeywell.

have specifically authorized the use of this material in whole or in part in the COBOL specifications. Such authorization extends to the reproduction and use of COBOL specifications in programming manuals or similar publications.

Table of Contents

Chapter 3 ADIS (continued)

Chapter 4 COBOL File Handling

Chapter 5 Compiler Directives

Chapter 6 Run Time System Error Messages

Index

Preface

COBOL is the computer language that Grace Murray Hopper created almost 40 years ago specifically for developing business applications. Rear Admiral Grace Murray Hopper was a Professor of Mathematics at Vassar when the U. S. Navy recruited her in 1943 to work on the first computer in the United States, the Mark I, at Harvard. There she built the first computer to translate mathematical notations into machine code. During the course of her work, Admiral Hopper created and standardized many key technical developments. The most notable was COBOL (Common Business Oriented Language) – the business programming language of choice – from the earliest computer into the age of the microchip and the World Wide Web.

Today in the era of distributed computing, e-business, the Internet and Personal Computers, COBOL remains the best choice for business application development. When you program with COBOL, you are part of a vast group of highly sought after software professionals. There are approximately 2.4 million COBOL programmers, maintaining and writing over 9.5 million COBOL applications. This represents over 60 percent of the world's computer code.

MERANT Micro Focus, the leading provider of COBOL tools and enterprise business solutions, was the first to bring COBOL to the Personal Computer desktop. As we move into the new millennium with emphasis on Web access and e-business, MERANT Micro Focus continues to be a leader in moving COBOL to these new topologies. Micro Focus software enables customers to accelerate e-business by maintaining, transforming and extending legacy business applications rapidly with low risk and high return on investment.

MERANT realizes that today's information students require knowledge and experience with the advanced computer technology being used by their prospective employers. The offering of this COBOL Reference Manual is evidence of the continuing commitment of MERANT Micro Focus to the teaching and learning of COBOL. The manual is an ideal addition for educational institutions, training organizations and self-learners who need a desk reference for the COBOL language. Whether you are a first time COBOL programmer or an experienced programmer this is an excellent book to add to your reference library.

Good luck and enjoy your learning experience.

Paul Halpern Ph.D.
MERANT Micro Focus
Academic Programs (academics@merant.com)

COBOL Reference Manual

Chapter 1

Language Reference

Overview

This Language Reference provides basic information about COBOL language syntax. When editing a program, you can get onscreen information by placing the cursor on a COBOL word and pressing **Alt F1**. The On-line Reference information will display either the function of the word with a syntax diagram of its use or a table of contents from which to select a topic.

COBOL Syntax

Personal COBOL Program Source

A COBOL program can consist of four divisions:

1. Identification Division - an identification of the program.

2. Environment Division - a description of the equipment to be used to compile and run the program.

3. Data Division - a description of the data to be processed.

4. Procedure Division - a set of procedures to specify the operations to be performed on the data.

Each division is divided into sections which are further divided into paragraphs, which in turn are made up of sentences.

In ANSI 85 COBOL the Identification Division must be included in every program, but the Environment, Data and Procedure Divisions may be omitted. In Micro Focus COBOL, the Identification Division may also be omitted. Personal COBOL will accept a program that contains only the sections and divisions that are necessary to the program.

Syntax Diagram Conventions

COBOL syntax is shown using diagrams called "railroad tracks", in which the words and phrases comprising a construct are shown joined by lines indicating the order they should be written in. You read these diagrams left-to-right. Each diagram starts with ▶▶ and ends with ▶◀.

Sometimes the track forks to show alternatives and then joins up again. An arrow starting after a word or phrase and pointing back before it, forming a loop, means it can be repeated. The length of a track has no significance.

When a diagram reaches the right-hand side of the page, it is continued further down. A track continued onto a new line ends with ▶, and the new line begins with ▶. If several tracks are are continued they are numbered so you can match up each track with its continuation.

Within the diagrams, COBOL reserved words which are not significant and can be left out without affecting the sense of the statement (noise words) are indicated by a "drop-out" with narrow sides. Reserved words which are optional, but change the sense of the statement when included are shown by a drop-out with wide sides. For example, in the statement:

the word NEW can be left out without affecting the operation. However, omitting the word BACKWARDS will produce a different effect than if it is included.

COBOL Syntax Diagrams

Construct: COBOL Source Program

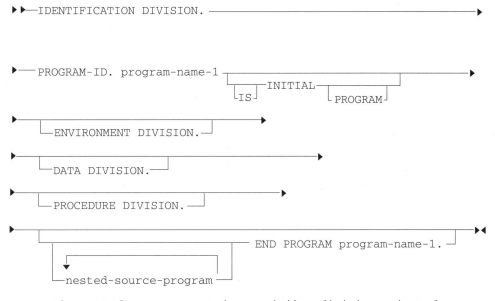

the nested program contains a similar division oriented structure.

Construct: Identification Division

Function: Identifies the program and contains documentry information about it.

Syntax:

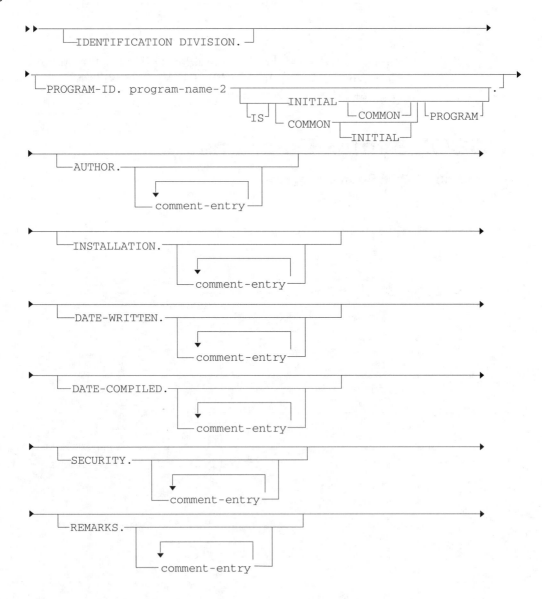

Construct: Environment Division

Function: Links names used in the program to external objects and selects options of the COBOL environment.

Syntax:

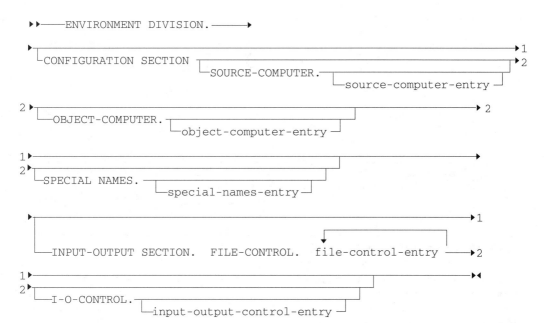

Construct: Source-computer Paragraph

Function: Describes the computer where the program is to be compiled, and enables debugging code.

Syntax:

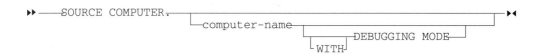

Construct: Object-computer Paragraph

Function: Describes the computer where the program is to run, and selects some options of the COBOL environment.

Syntax:

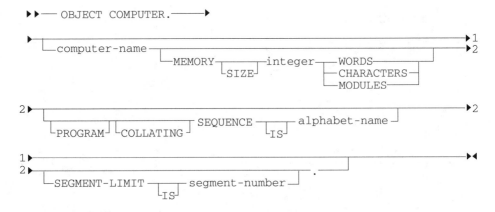

Construct: Special-names Paragraph

Function: Links names used in the program to external switches, and selects some options of the COBOL environment.

Syntax:

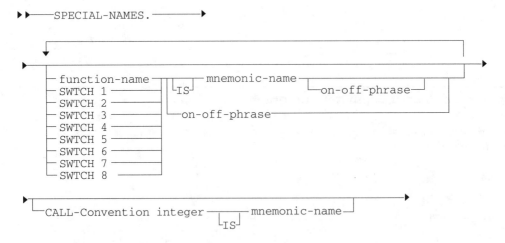

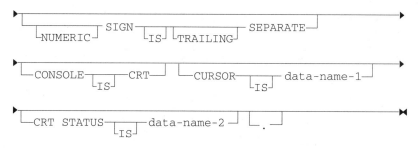

where on-off phrase is:

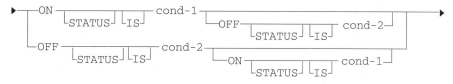

Construct: Input-Output Section

Function: Gives details of files and specifies file handling options.

Syntax:

Construct: File-control Entry (SELECT)

Function: Assigns names to files, for use in the program, and describes the files.

Syntax: Sequential.

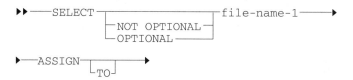

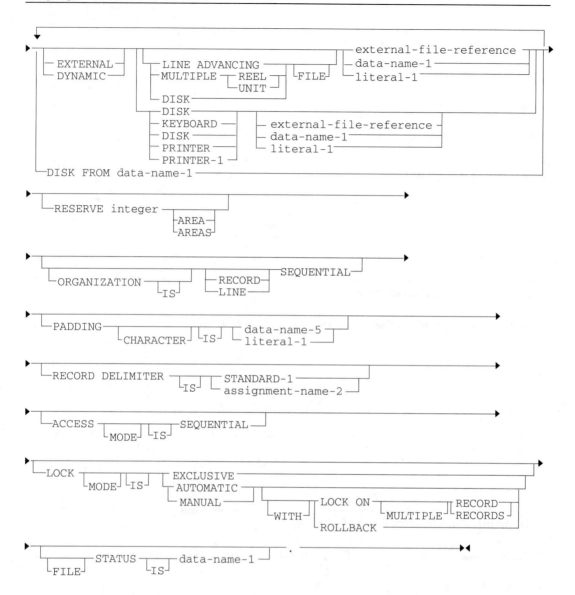

Construct: File-control Entry (SELECT)

Function: Assigns names to files, for use in the program, and describes the files.

Syntax: Relative.

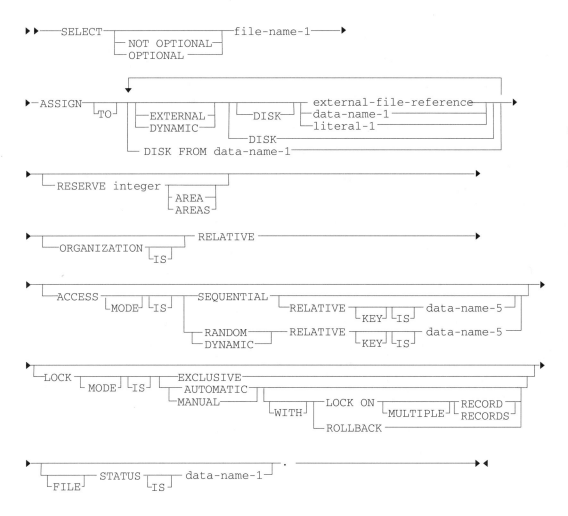

Construct: File-control Entry (SELECT)

Function: Assigns names to files, for use in the program, and describes the files.

Syntax: Indexed.

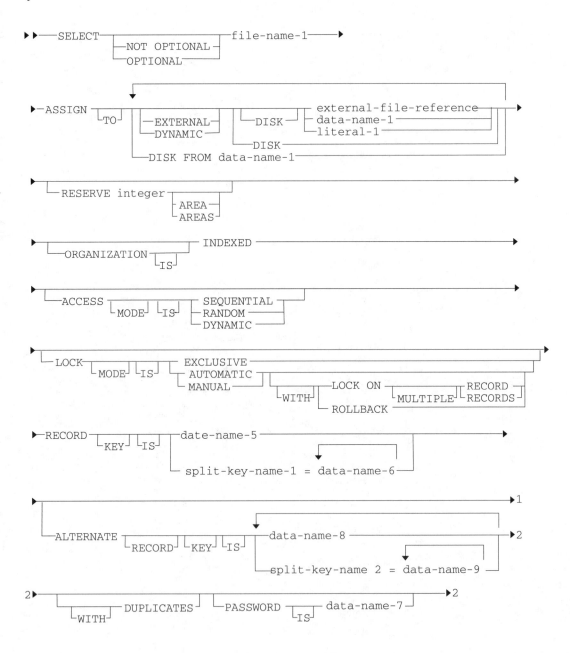

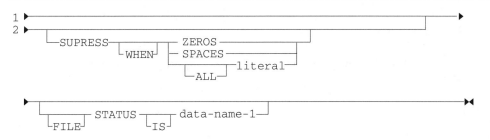

Construct: File-control Entry (SELECT)

Function: Assigns names to files, for use in the program, and describes the files.

Syntax: Sort-merge.

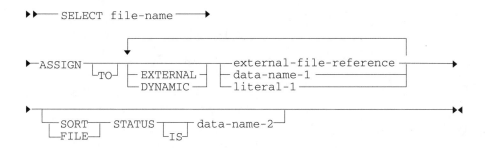

Construct: I-O-Control Paragraph

Function: Specifies file-handling options.

Syntax:

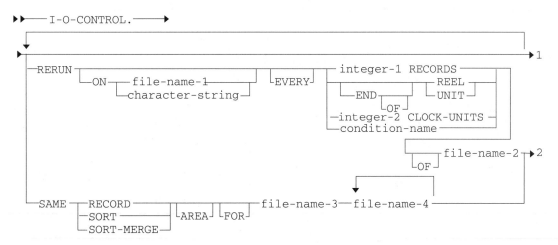

Language Reference

Construct: Data Division

Function: Defines the data that the program is to accept as input, work on internally, or produce as output.

Syntax:

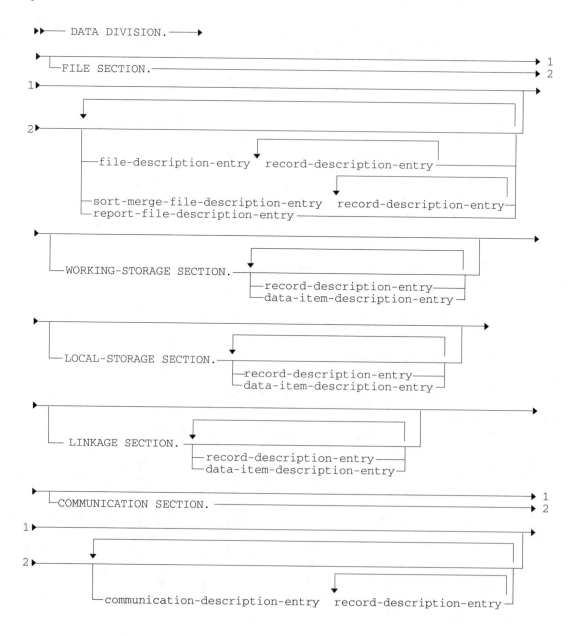

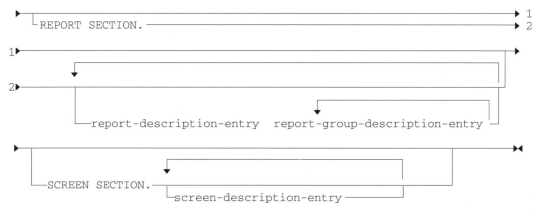

Construct: File Description Entry (FD)

See also:

Sort-merge file Description Entry.

Function: Gives further details of a file (in addition to the information in the File-control paragraph) and begins the descriptions of its record layouts.

Syntax: Please see the On-line Reference for specific syntax in a given instance.

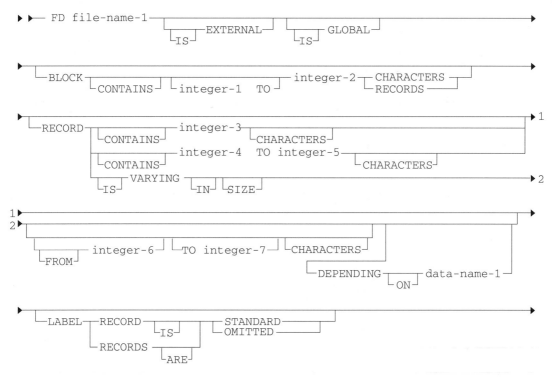

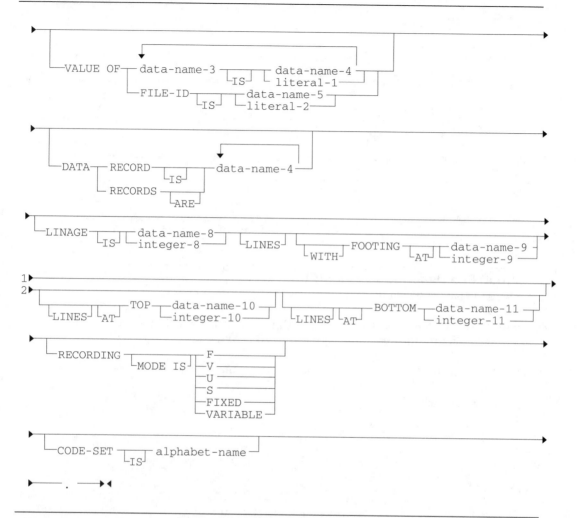

Construct: Sort-Merge File Description Entry (SD)

Function: Gives further details of a Sort-Merge file (in addition to the information in File-control paragraph) and begins the descriptions of its record layouts.

Syntax:

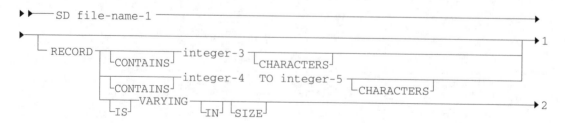

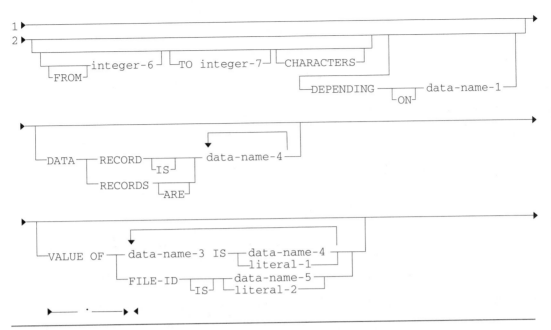

Construct: Data Description Entry

Function: Reserves and names an area of memory for storing an item of data, and describes the data to be stored there.

Syntax:

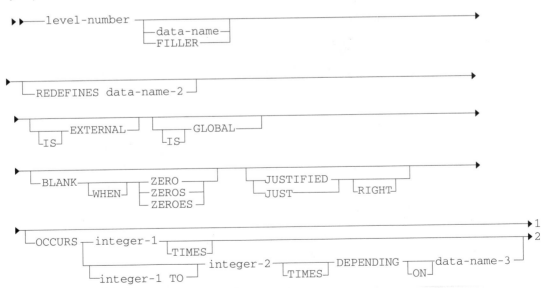

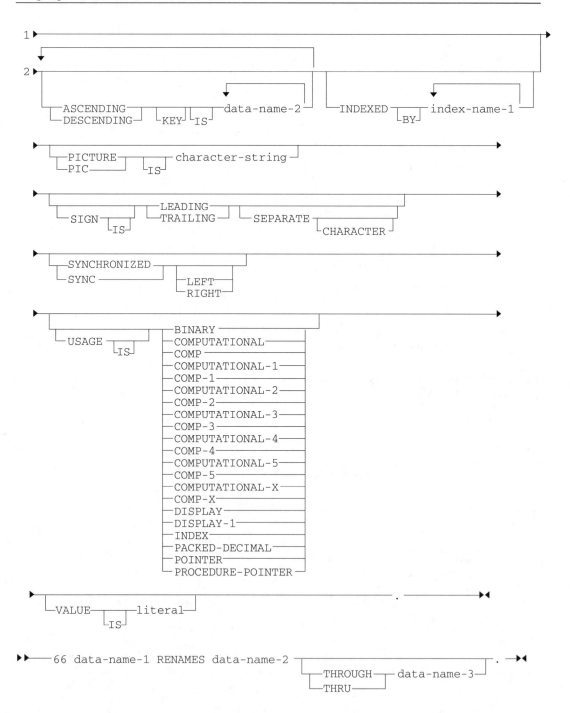

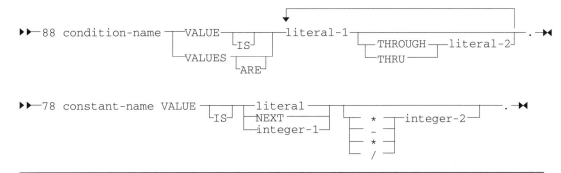

Construct: Screen Description Entry

Function: Reserves and names an area of the screen for displaying or accepting an item of data, and describes the data to be displayed or accepted there.

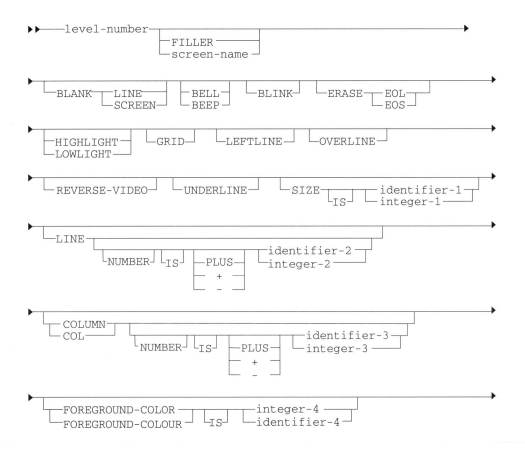

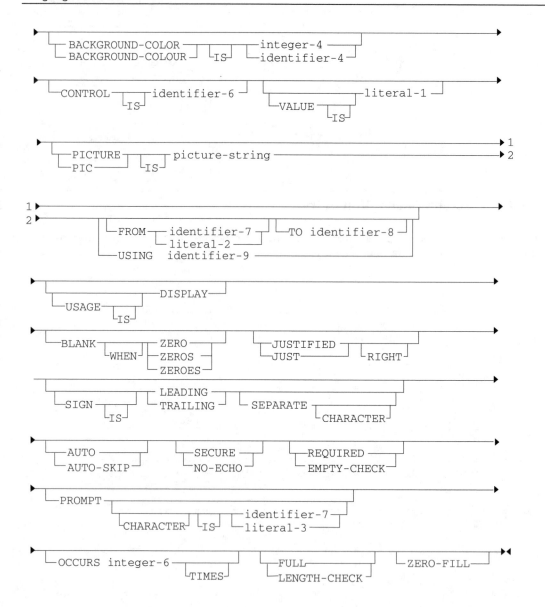

Construct: **Procedure Division**

Function: Contains the executable statements of the program.

Syntax: Please see the On-line Reference for specific syntax in a given instance.

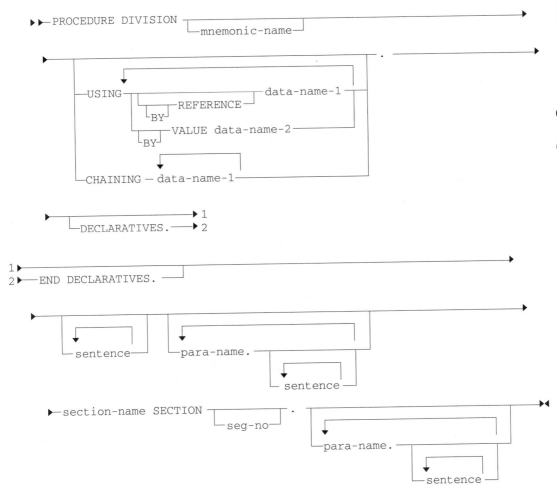

Construct: ACCEPT

Function: Gets data from a physical device, such as the keyboard, or from the operating system.

Syntax 1: Line at a time.

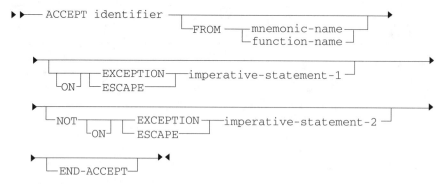

Syntax 2: From DATE etc.

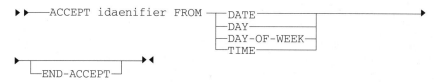

Syntax 3: Screen item.

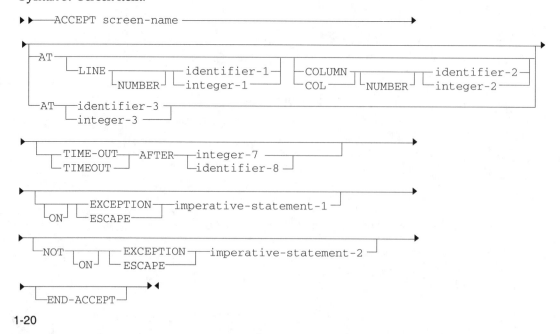

Syntax 4: Full screen.

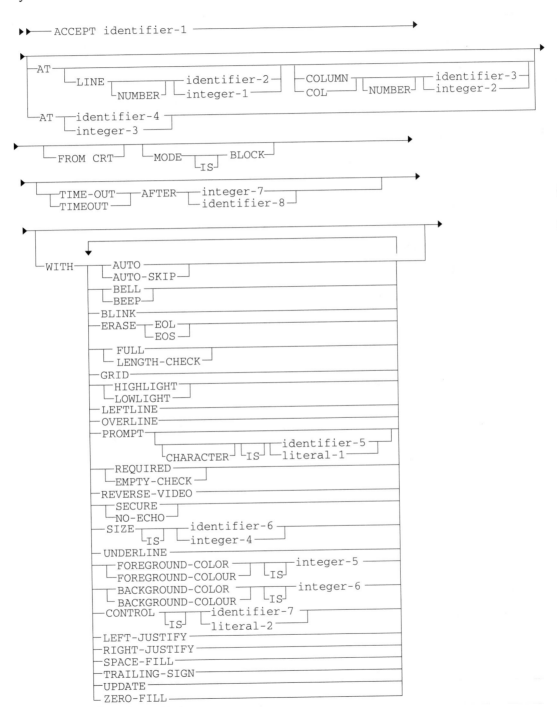

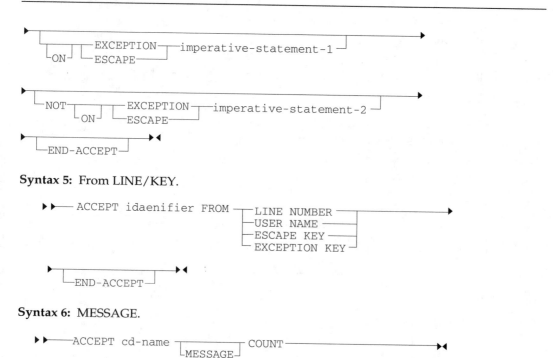

Syntax 5: From LINE/KEY.

```
►►── ACCEPT idaenifier FROM ──┬─ LINE NUMBER ──────┬──────►
                              ├─ USER NAME ─────────┤
                              ├─ ESCAPE KEY ────────┤
                              └─ EXCEPTION KEY ──────┘
```

```
►─────────────────────►◄
    └─ END-ACCEPT ──┘
```

Syntax 6: MESSAGE.

```
►►── ACCEPT cd-name ──┬──────────┬── COUNT ──────────►◄
                      └─ MESSAGE ─┘
```

Verb: ADD

Function: Adds two or more numeric operands and stores the result.

Syntax 1: Simple.

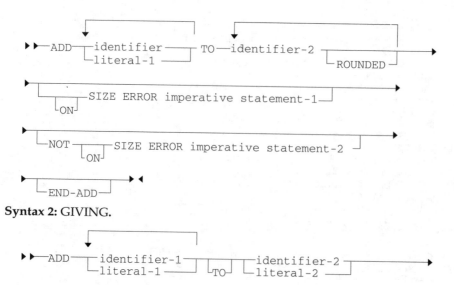

```
►─────────────────────────────────────────────────►
   └─┬──┐ ─ SIZE ERROR imperative statement-1 ──┘
     └ON┘
```

```
►─────────────────────────────────────────────────►
   └─ NOT ─┬──┐ ─ SIZE ERROR imperative statement-2 ──┘
           └ON┘
```

```
►─────────────────────►◄
   └─ END-ADD ─┘
```

Syntax 2: GIVING.

```
                    ┌──────────────┐
►►── ADD ──┬─ identifier-1 ─┬──┬────┬─┬─ identifier-2 ─┬──────►
           └─ literal-1 ────┘  └ TO ┘ └─ literal-2 ────┘
```

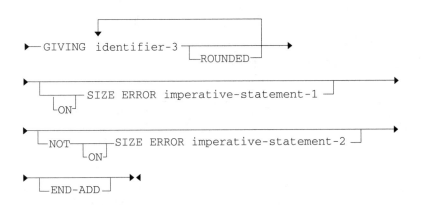

Syntax 3: CORRESPONDING.

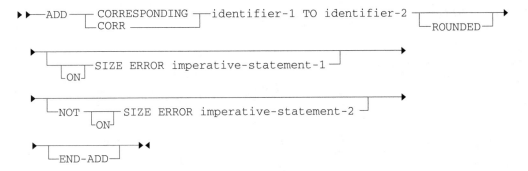

Verb: **ALTER**

Function: Modifies a predetermined sequence of operations.

Syntax:

Verb: **CALL**

Function: Transfers control to another program in the run unit, with automatic return of control when that program finishes.

Syntax 1: OVERFLOW.

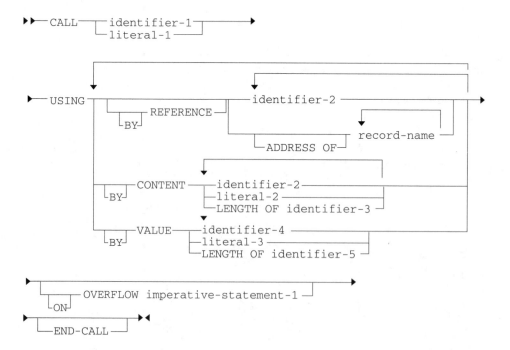

Syntax: EXCEPTION.

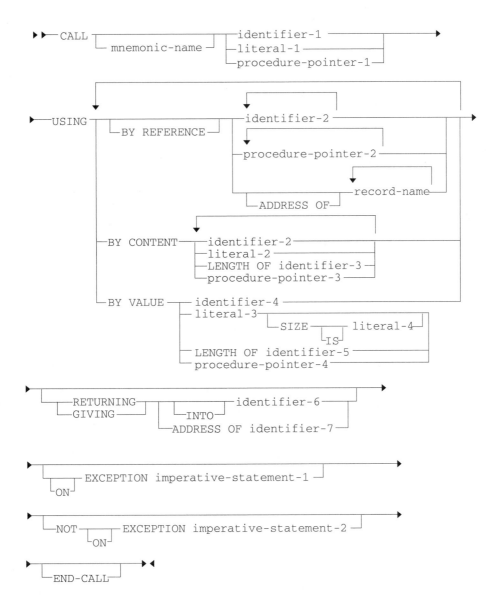

Verb: CANCEL

Function: Ensures that the next time the program referenced is called it will be in its initial state.

Syntax:

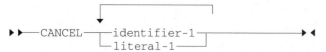

Verb: CHAIN

Function: Transfers control to another program in the run-unit, with no subsequent return of control.

Syntax:

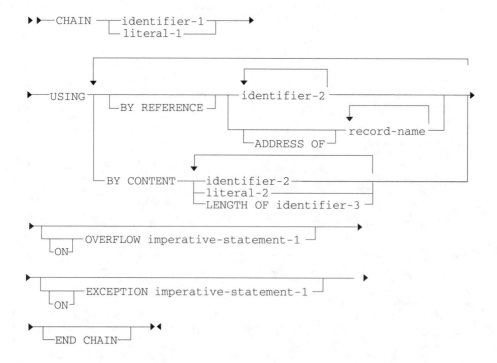

Construct: **Class Condition**

Function: Tests class of data item.

Syntax:

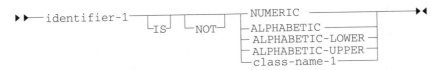

Verb: **CLOSE**

Function: Terminates the processing of files.

Syntax:

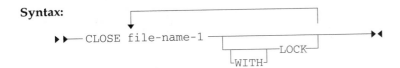

Verb: **COMPUTE**

Function: Evaluates an arithmetic expression and stores the result.

Syntax:

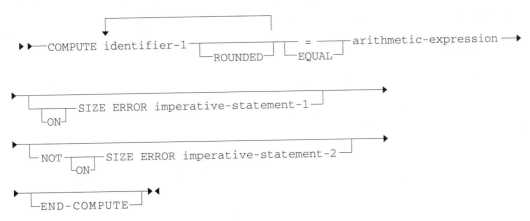

Verb: CONTINUE

Function: No effect. Used where no operation is wanted but COBOL syntax requires a verb.

Syntax:

Construct: COPY Statement

Function: Include separate text files with optional string replacement.

Syntax:

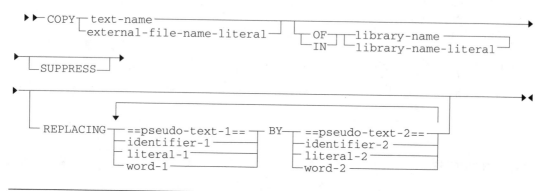

Verb: DELETE

Function: Deletes a record from a relative or indexed file, or deletes files from the devices they are on.

Syntax 1: RECORD.

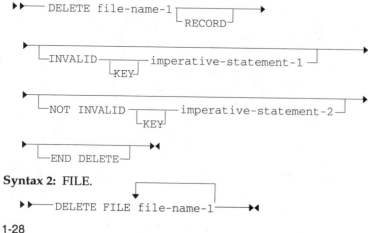

Syntax 2: FILE.

```
▶▶────DELETE FILE file-name-1────▶◀
```

Verb: DISPLAY

Function: Sends data to a physical device, such as the screen..

Syntax 1: Line at a time.

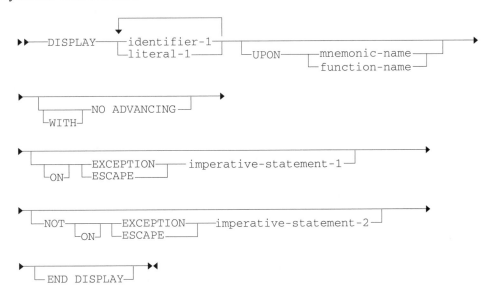

Syntax 2: Screen item.

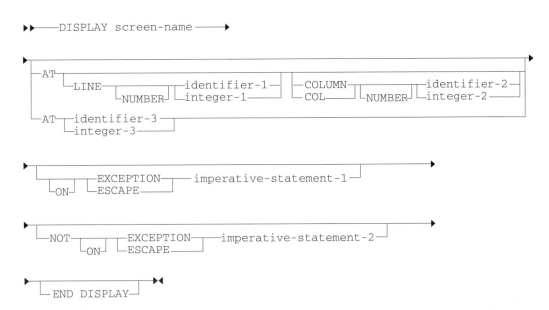

Syntax 3: Full screen.

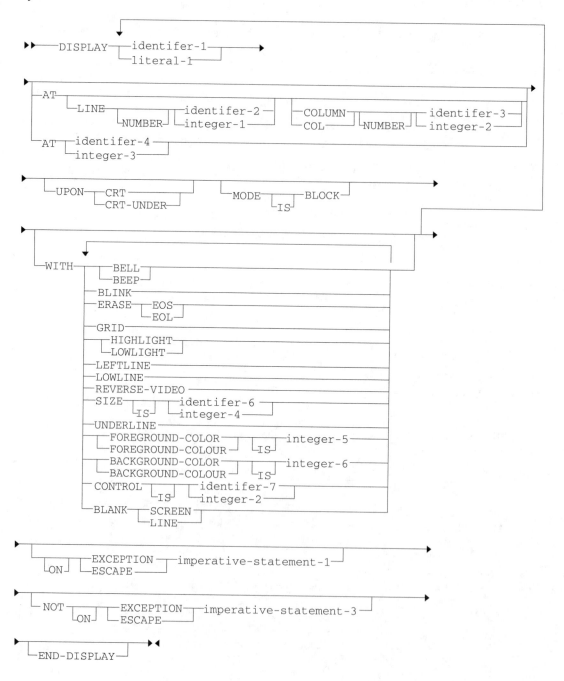

Verb: DIVIDE

Function: Divides one numeric data item into another and stores the quotient and remainder.

Syntax 1: Simple.

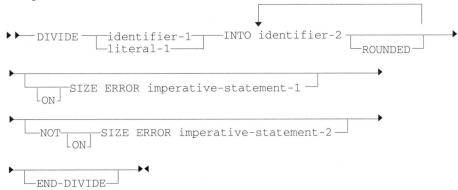

Syntax 2: INTO GIVING.

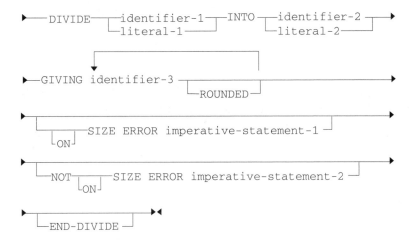

Syntax 3: BY GIVING.

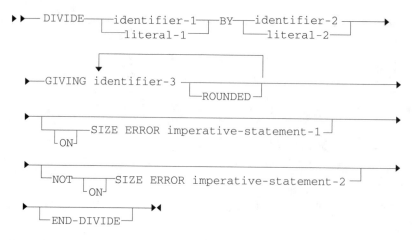

Syntax 4: INTO REMAINDER.

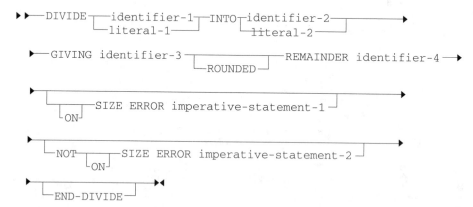

Syntax 5: BY REMAINDER.

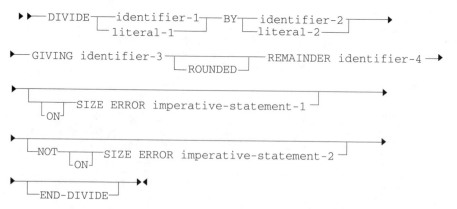

Verb: **ENTER**

Function: Allows the use of another language in a COBOL program.

General Rule: This statement is treated as for documentation purposes only and is not executed.

Syntax:

Verb: **EVALUATE**

Function: Tests multiple conditions and executes a different branch depending on the result.

Syntax:

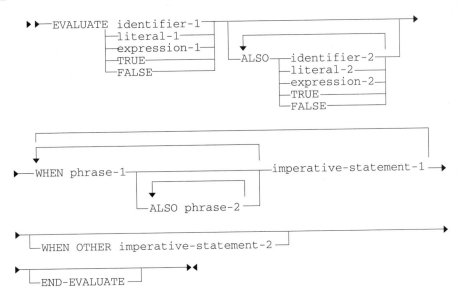

where phrase-1 is:

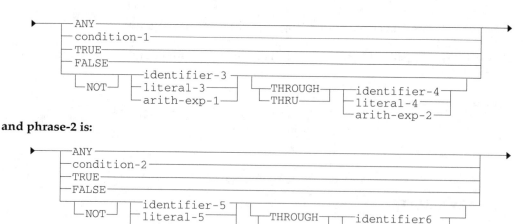

and phrase-2 is:

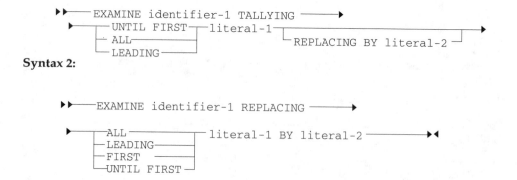

Verb: **EXAMINE**

Function: Replaces or counts the occurrences of a given character in a data item.

Syntax 1:

```
►►——EXAMINE identifier-1 TALLYING ——►
    ►—┬─UNTIL FIRST─┬─literal-1─┬────────────────────────┬──►
      ├─ ALL────────┘           └─REPLACING BY literal-2─┘
      └─ LEADING────┘
```

Syntax 2:

```
►►——EXAMINE identifier-1 REPLACING ——►
    ►—┬─ALL──────┬─literal-1 BY literal-2 ——►◄
      ├─LEADING──┤
      ├─FIRST ───┤
      └─UNTIL FIRST─┘
```

Verb: **EXHIBIT**

Function: Displays data items, optionally preceded by their identifiers, and literals. The display can be conditional.

Syntax:

Verb: **EXIT**

Function: Marks the end of a procedure or cycle of an in-line perform, causing the indicated level of procedure (PERFORM CYCLE, PERFORM, PARAGRAPH, SECTION or PRO-GRAM) to be terminated at that point.

Syntax 1: PROGRAM.

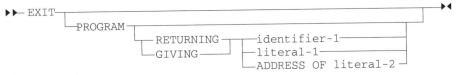

Syntax 2: PERFORM.

Syntax 3: PARAGRAPH.

Verb: GO TO

Function: Transfers control elsewhere in the Procedure Division.

Syntax 1:

Syntax 2:

Verb: GOBACK

Function: Transfers control to the calling program, or to the operating system if the program was not called.

Syntax:

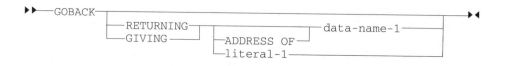

Verb: IF

Function: Tests a condition and executes a different branch depending on the result.

Syntax:

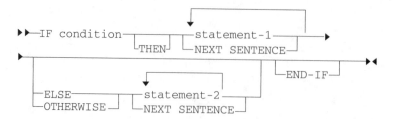

Verb: **INITIALIZE**

Function: Assigns values to all data items of a specified type that are subordinate to a specified data item.

Syntax:

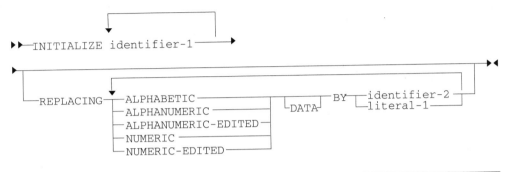

Verb: **INSPECT**

Function: Counts, replaces, or converts occurrences of a character or group of characters in a data item.

Syntax 1: TALLYING.

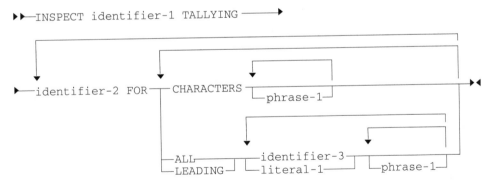

where phrase-1 is:

Syntax 2: REPLACING.

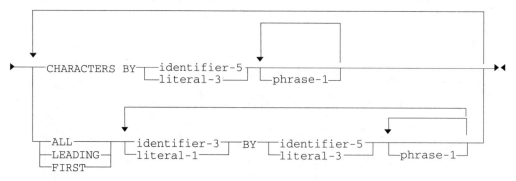

where phrase-1 is:

Syntax 3: TALLYING REPLACING.

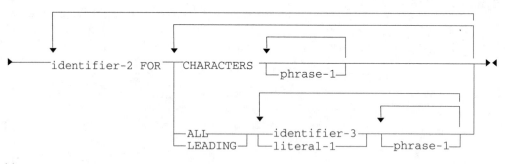

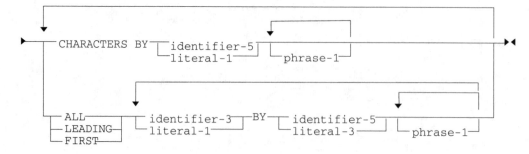

where phrase-1 is:

Syntax 4: CONVERTING.

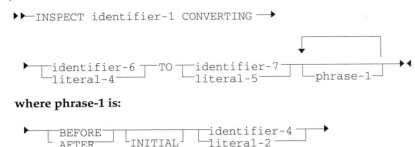

where phrase-1 is:

Verb: MERGE

Function: Combines two or more identically sequenced files on a set of specified keys, and passes the records, in merge order, to an output procedure or output file.

Syntax:

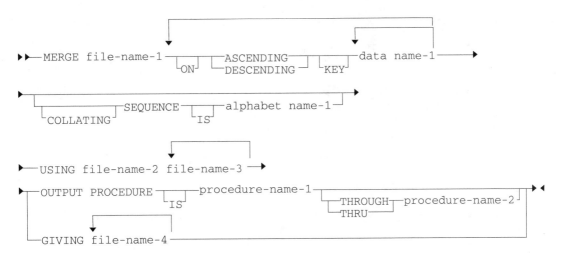

Verb: MOVE

Function: Copies data from one data item to others, in accordance with editing rules.

Syntax 1: Simple.

Syntax 2: Corresponding.

Verb: MULTIPLY

Function: Multiplies numeric data items and stores the result.

Syntax 1: Simple.

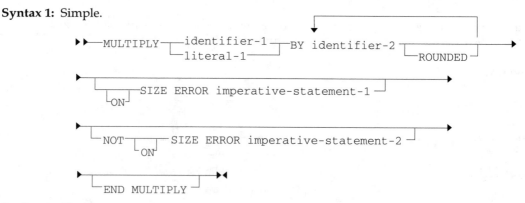

Syntax 2: Giving.

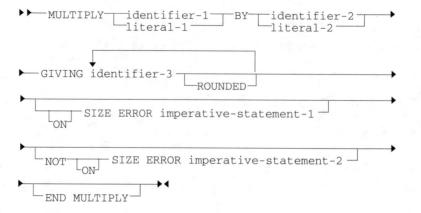

Verb: ON

Function: Causes a group of statements to be executed periodically.

Syntax:

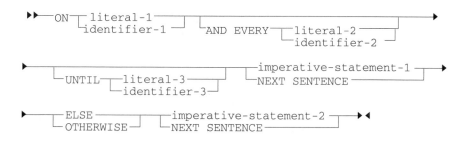

Verb: OPEN

Function: Initiates the processing of files. It checks and/or writes labels and does other related tasks.

Syntax 1: Sequential.

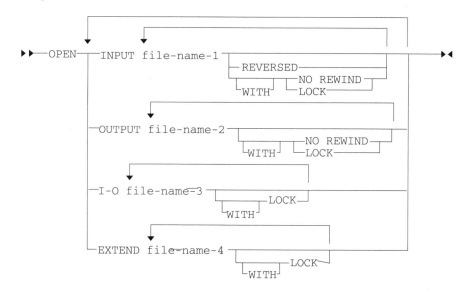

Syntax 2: Relative and indexed.

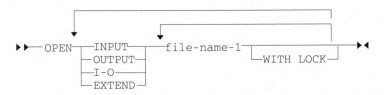

Verb: PERFORM

Function: Causes a group of statements to be executed repeatedly. If the statements are a procedure, this statement repeatedly transfers control to that procedure, with automatic return of control each time the procedure finishes.

Syntax 1: Simple.

```
▶▶─PERFORM ┬─procedure-name-1───────────────────────────────────────────┬─▶◀
           │                    ┌─THROUGH─┬─procedure-name-2 ─┐          │
           │                    └─THRU────┘                    │          │
           └─imperative statement END-PERFORM ─────────────────────────────┘
```

Syntax 2: TIMES.

```
▶▶─PERFORM ┬─procedure-name-1──────────────────────────────────────┬─phrase─▶
           │                  ┌─THROUGH─┬─procedure-name-2 ─┐       │
           │                  └─THRU────┘                    │       │
           └─phrase─imperative statement END-PERFORM ─────────────────┘
```

where phrase is:

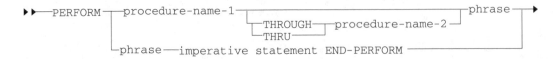

Syntax 3: UNTIL.

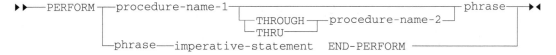

where phrase is:

Syntax 4: VARYING.

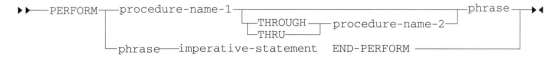

where phrase is:

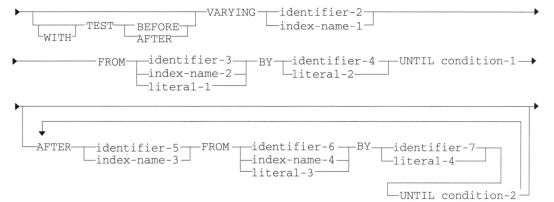

Construct: Pointer Condition

Function: Compares pointer items.

Syntax:

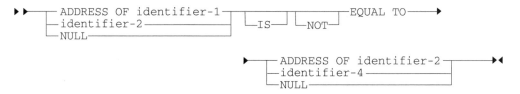

Language Reference

Construct: Qualification

Function: Identifies which item is meant out of several with the same name.

Syntax 1: Data division names.

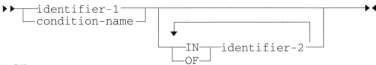

Syntax 2: LINAGE.

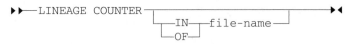

Syntax 3: Procedure division names.

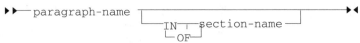

Syntax 4: COPY Library.

Verb: READ

Function: Gets a record from a file. In sequential access this will be the next or previous record; in random access, it will be a specified record.

Syntax 1: Sequential.

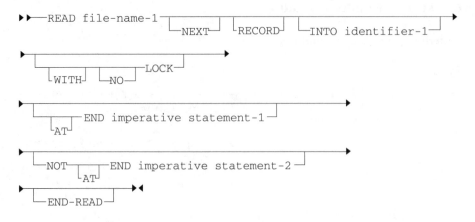

Syntax 2: NEXT/PREVIOUS.

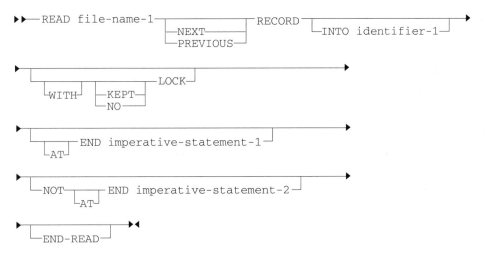

Syntax 3: Relative key.

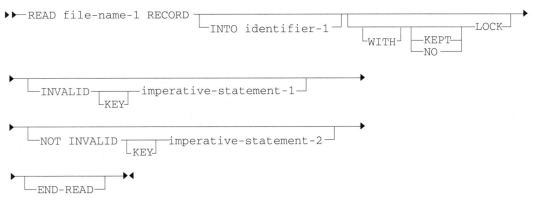

Syntax 4: Record key.

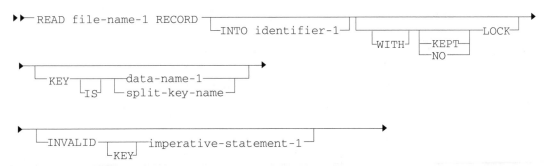

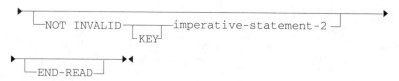

Verb: **READY**

Function: Enter trace mode.

Syntax:

▶▶──READY-TRACE──────────────────────────▶◀

CONSTRUCT: **Relation Condition**

Function: Comparision between data items.

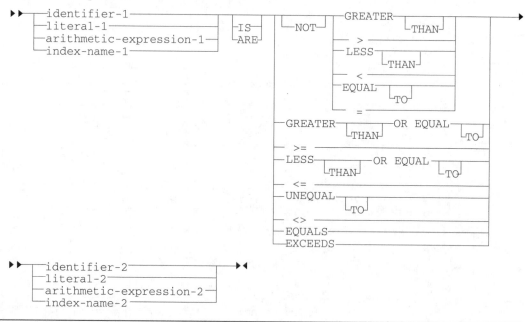

Verb: **RELEASE**

Function: Passes records to the initial phase of a sort operation.

Syntax:

▶▶──RELEASE record-name ──────────────▶◀
                        └─FROM identifier-1─┘

Construct: REPLACE Statement

Function: Replace text in source lines.

Syntax:

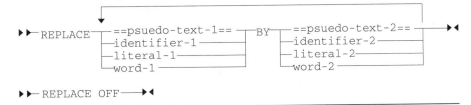

Verb: RESET

Function: End trace mode.

Syntax: ▶▶─ RESET TRACE ─────────────────▶◀

Verb: RETURN

Function: Gets records from the final phase of a sort operation or merged records during a merge operation.

Syntax:

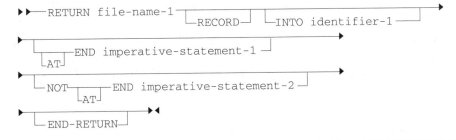

Verb: REWRITE

Function: Replaces an existing record in a file with an updated copy of the same record.

Syntax: Please see the On-line Reference for specific syntax in a given instance.

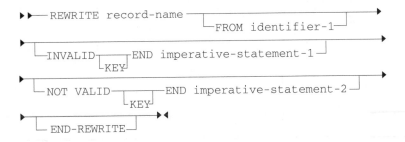

Language Reference

Verb: **SEARCH**

Function: Searches a table for an element satisfying a given condition and sets the associated index-name to point to it.

Syntax 1: Simple.

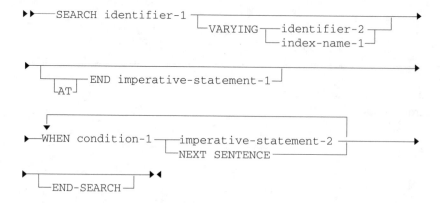

Syntax 2: All.

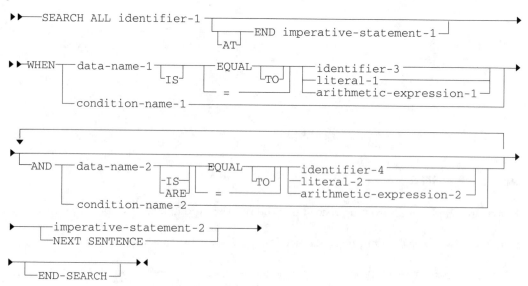

Verb: SET

Function: Assigns a value to an item of a type used for program control rather than data storage; that is index name, condition-name, switch, or data item of USAGE INDEX, POINTER or PROCEDURE-POINTER>

Syntax 1: Index.

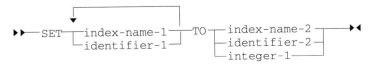

Syntax 2: Index UP/DOWN.

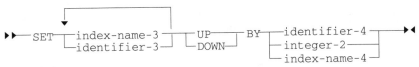

Syntax 3: Condition-name.

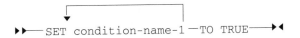

Syntax 4: Switch.

Syntax 5: Address.

Syntax 6: Pointer UP/DOWN.

Syntax 7: Procedure pointer.

Construct: Sign Condition

Function: Tests sign of data item.

Syntax:

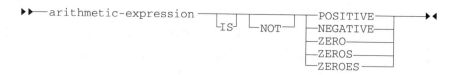

Verb: SORT

Function: Sorts records into order on a set of specified keys. These records can come from a file or from a table, or be created by an input procedure.

Syntax 1:

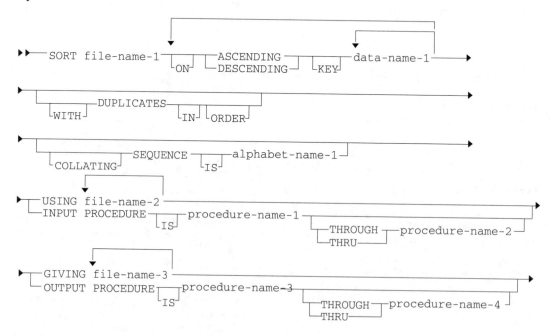

Syntax 2: Table.

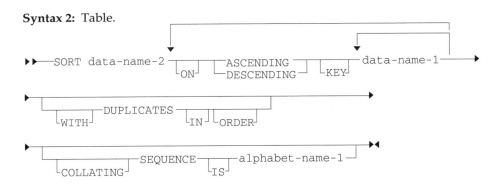

Verb: **START**

Function: Positions a relative or indexed file for subsequent retrieval of records.

Syntax 1: Relative.

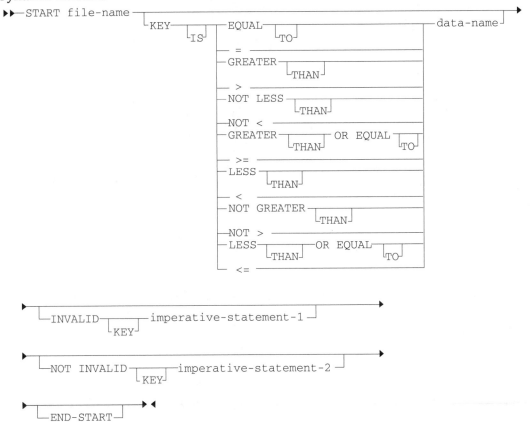

Syntax 2: Indexed.

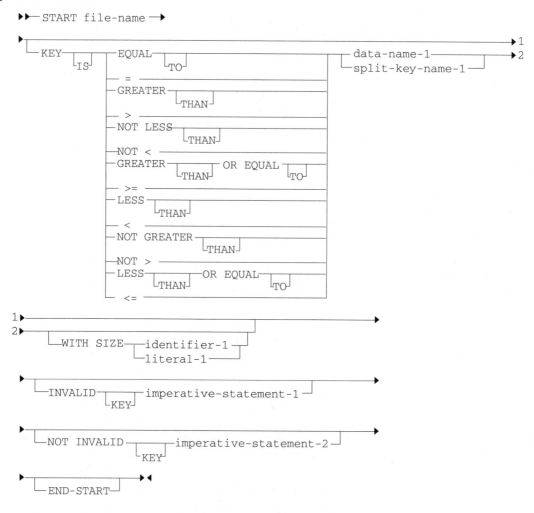

Verb: STOP

Function: Suspends execution of the program, either permanently or temporarily.

Syntax:

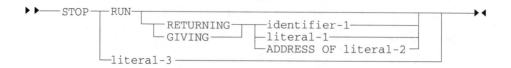

Verb: **STRING**

Function: Concatenates the partial or complete contents of two or more data items and stores the result.

Syntax:

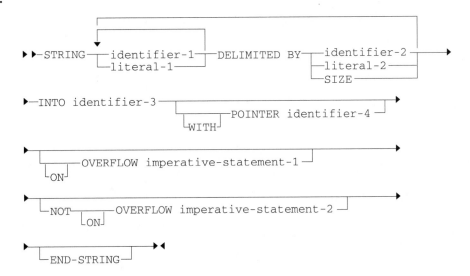

Verb: **SUBTRACT**

Function: Subtracts one or more numeric data items from another and stores the result.

Syntax 1: Simple.

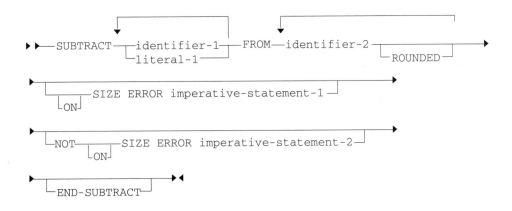

Syntax 2: GIVING.

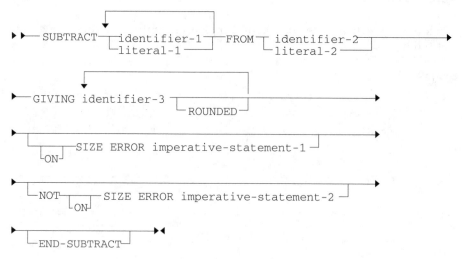

Syntax 3: CORRESPONDING.

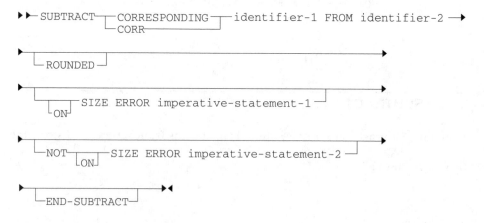

Construct: Subscripting

Function: Identifies which element of a table is meant.

Syntax:

Verb: **UNSTRING**

Function: Splits the contents of a data item into separate character strings and stores them.

Syntax:

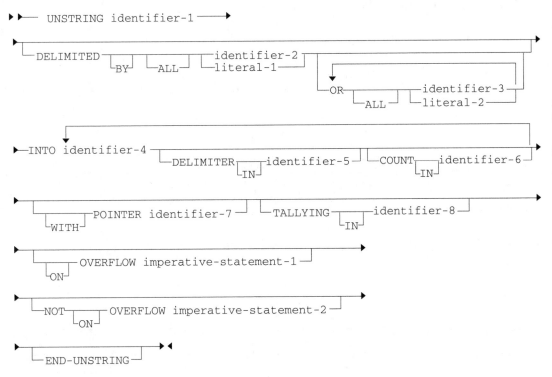

Verb: USE

Function: Causes the section it introduces to be executed whenever specified circumstances arise. Control may transfer itself to that section from any point in the Procedure Division, with automatic return of control when the section finishes. This statement introduces sections in the Declaratives that handle file errors, etc.; the section it introduces is executed only if the file in error has a file status item.

Syntax 1: ERROR/EXCEPTION.

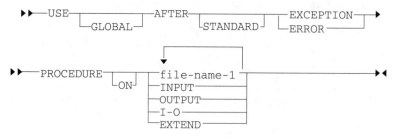

Syntax 2: Reporting.

Syntax 3: DEBUGGING.

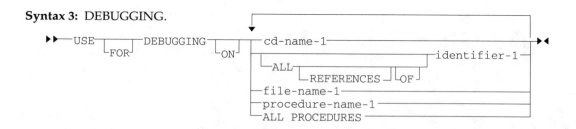

Verb: **WRITE**

Function: Sends a record to a file. For a sequential file this statement can also position lines vertically on the page.

Syntax 1: ADVANCING.

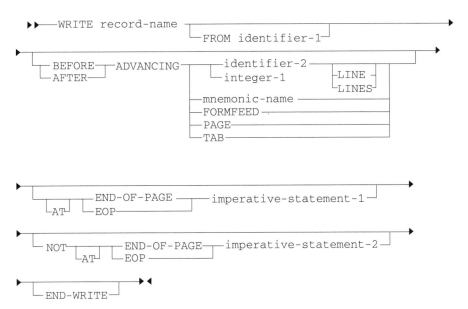

Syntax 2: INVALID KEY.

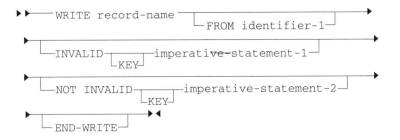

Chapter 2

COBOL Library Routines

The Personal COBOL System includes a built-in library of routines which programs can use. The library routines are available using the COBOL CALL statement, and generally supply features that are not provided by the COBOL language. The library routines with names that begin "CBL" are in all current MERANT Micro Focus COBOL products.

Overview

The library routines supplied with the run-time system in Personal COBOL supply features not provided by COBOL syntax, such as operating system functions.

In some cases, the call-by-name and call-by-number routines are interchangeable. For each call-by-number routine there may be a corresponding call-by-name routine. There are also many additional call-by-name routines. These routines may have functionality not found in the corresponding call-by-number routines. You are encouraged to use call-by-name routines rather than call-by-number routines where possible.

Call-by-Name Routines

To use a library routine, use the name of the required routine in a CALL statement with parameters as shown in the description of the routine.

Routines by Category

Routines by Category is intended to help find routines for particular purposes. Functions are listed by name and organized into categories (with a very brief description of the purpose of each). The section *Descriptions of Routines* contains complete descriptions of the routines, listed in alphabetical order.

The categories of call-by-name routines are:

■ Byte-Stream Files

■ Closedown Procedure

■ File-names

■ Files

■ Keyboard

■ Logic Operators

■ Mouse

■ Printer

■ Screen

■ Text

The routines in each category are listed below. Details common to all the routines in a category are also shown.

Byte-Stream Files

CBL_CLOSE_FILE	Closes a file
CBL_CREATE_FILE	Create byte-stream file
CBL_OPEN_FILE	Open byte-stream file
CBL_READ_FILE	Read byte-stream file
CBL_WRITE_FILE	Write byte-stream file

The Micro Focus byte-stream file routines allow you to read and write data files without the need to adhere to COBOL record definitions.

For all these routines, if the routine is successful the RETURN-CODE register will be set to zero. If the routine fails, the RE-TURN-CODE register will contain a file status value indicating the failure. This file status will always be the standard ANSI '74 file status value. If no ANSI '74 file status is defined for the error, a standard Micro Focus error status will be returned (9/*nnn* where *nnn* is the RTS error number).

Closedown Procedure

PC_EXIT_PROC   Register closedown procedure

File-names

CBL_JOIN_FILENAME   Join parts of file-name
CBL_SPLIT_FILENAME   Divide file-name into parts

These routines enable you to parse a file-name into its component strings and to join strings together to form a file-name. They can be used together to replace components of a file-name, such as the extension. They can handle both null-terminated and space-terminated file-names.

A file-name is split up into device, base-name and extension. For example, in the following file-name:

d:\dir1\dir2\file.dat

The device is *d:\dir1\dir2*, the base-name is *file*, and the extension is *dat*. The maximum length of the file name string is 65 characters.

Files

CBL_CHANGE_DIR   Change current directory
CBL_CHECK_FILE_EXIST   Check if file exists

Library Routines

CBL_COPY_FILE	Copy file
CBL_CREATE_DIR	Create directory
CBL_DELETE_DIR	Delete directory
CBL_DELETE_FILE	Delete file
CBL_READ_DIR	Read current directory
CBL_RENAME_FILE	Rename file
PC_FIND_DRIVES	Find valid drives
PC_LOCATE_FILE	Locate file/expand path
PC_READ_DRIVE	Read current drive
PC_SET_DRIVE	Set current drive

Keyboard

CBL_GET_KBD_STATUS	Test for character at keyboard
CBL_READ_KBD_CHAR	Read character from keyboard (no echo)

Logic Operators

CBL_AND	Logical AND
CBL_EQ	Logical EQuivalence
CBL_IMP	Logical IMPlies
CBL_NOT	Logical NOT
CBL_OR	Logical OR
CBL_XOR	Logical eXclusive OR

These routines carry out logic operations on bits. Apart from CBL_NOT, all these operations have two operands.

In the two-operand routines, interchanging the two operands, source and target, does not change the result except in CBL_IMP. However, the result is always stored in the second operand, target.

If *length* is longer than either data item, bytes following that data item will be used, up to the length specified. This could overwrite program data.

The parameter *length* can be replaced by the syntax:

length of *source*

or

length of *target*

assuming all the bytes of the data item are to be used.

Mouse

CBL_GET_MOUSE_MASK	Get mouse event mask
CBL_GET_MOUSE_POSITION	Get mouse screen coordinates
CBL_GET_MOUSE_STATUS	Get number of events in queue
CBL_HIDE_MOUSE	Hide mouse pointer
CBL_INIT_MOUSE	Initialize mouse support
CBL_READ_MOUSE_EVENT	Read mouse event queue
CBL_SET_MOUSE_MASK	Set mouse event mask
CBL_SET_MOUSE_POSITION	Set mouse screen coordinates
CBL_SHOW_MOUSE	Draw mouse pointer
CBL_TERM_MOUSE	Terminate mouse support
PC_GET_MOUSE_SHAPE	Get mouse pointer shape
PC_SET_MOUSE_HIDE_AREA	Set mouse hide area
PC_SET_MOUSE_SHAPE	Set mouse pointer shape

Using the Routines

The mouse is useful for applications that require users to select from a list of options or move objects around on the screen.

To use these routines, you must have loaded a suitable mouse driver.

You must hide the mouse during the execution of any ANSI ACCEPT or DISPLAY statement that operates on the area of the screen where the mouse pointer is located.

The attributes referred to in the descriptions of routines are screen attributes, not user attributes. The top left-hand corner of the screen is row 0, column 0.

Mouse Events

Whenever the mouse is moved or a button on the mouse is pressed or released, the mouse hardware causes an interrupt. The mouse device driver takes control and, depending on a mask you have set, either saves it in a queue or ignores it. This prevents events being lost if a subsequent interrupt occurs before the application has read the event. With the mouse routines, you can read the event queue and determine how many events are in the queue.

When an event is generated, a description of it is stored in a data structure called the event-data. If the mask allows (see below), this is added to the queue. The layout of *event-data* is:

```
event-type   PIC X(2) COMP-X.
event-time   PIC X(4) COMP-X.
event-row    PIC X(2) COMP-X.
event-col    PIC X(2) COMP-X.
```

where:

event-type is the action (that is, change of state) that took place:

> bit 3 set   = button 3 pressed
> bit 2 set   = button 2 pressed
> bit 1 set   = button 1 pressed
> bit 0 set   = mouse moved
> (other bits are reserved.)

A button release is indicated by the bit for that button changing from 1 to 0. For example, if the mouse moves and button 1 is pressed at the same time, *event-type* contains 3.

event-time   is the time elapsed between when the event took place and some arbitrary but fixed starting time.

event-row   gives the row position of the mouse when the event took place.

event-col   gives the column position of the mouse when the event took place.

The Event Mask

The event mask, which the programmer supplies, tells the system which kinds of event should be queued and which ignored. It has the same structure as *event-type*. An event is queued only if it happens while the corresponding mask bit is on, or while another state is on whose mask bit is on. When an event-data is queued, the bit for each state is set correctly; that is, the mask does not mask them out.

For example, the operator moving the mouse will generate an event if either the mask bit for "mouse moved" is off or the operator is holding down a button and the mask bit for that button is off.

Printer

PC_TEST_PRINTER	Test printer status

Screen

CBL_CLEAR_SCR	Clear screen
CBL_GET_CSR_POS	Get cursor position
CBL_GET_SCR_SIZE	Get screen size
CBL_READ_SCR_ATTRS	Read attribute string
CBL_READ_SCR_CHARS	Read character string
CBL_READ_SCR_CHATTRS	Read character & attribute strings
CBL_SET_CSR_POS	Set cursor position
CBL_SWAP_SCR_CHATTRS	Swap character & attribute
CBL_WRITE_SCR_ATTRS	Write attribute string
CBL_WRITE_SCR_CHARS	Write character string
CBL_WRITE_SCR_CHARS_ATTR	Write character string with attribute
CBL_WRITE_SCR_CHATTRS	Write character & attribute strings
CBL_WRITE_SCR_TTY	Write characters TTY-style
CBL_WRITE_SCR_N_ATTR	Repeat write attribute
CBL_WRITE_SCR_N_CHAR	Repeat write character
CBL_WRITE_SCR_N_CHATTR	Repeat write character & attributes

Text

CBL_TOLOWER   Convert a string to lower case
CBL_TOUPPER   Convert a string to upper case

Descriptions of Routines

Descriptions for all of the call-by-name routines appear alphabetically.

Key

Each description contains the routine name and function and the entries (as appropriate) noted below.

Syntax:

Shows the CALL statement you could use to call the routine. The parameters you have to define are listed in the USING clause.

The optional RETURNING clause is also shown. Every routine returns a value showing the result of the operation. Unless otherwise indicated, zero indicates success, nonzero indicates failure. This value is left in the data item specified in the RETURNING clause - in this manual, *status-code*. If this clause is omitted, the value is left in the special register RETURN-CODE.

Parameters:

Describes any parameters shown in the RETURNING and USING clause. A parameter enclosed in brackets, for example, [parameter1] is optional and may not be needed for all forms of the routine.

Description:

Provides any additional information necessary for the successful use of the routine.

Parameters on Entry:

Indicates which of the parameters shown are passed on entry.

Parameters on Exit:

Indicates which of the parameters shown are returned on exit.

CBL_AND

Does a logical AND between the bits of two data items.

Syntax:

```
CALL "CBL_AND" USING source
                     target
               BY VALUE length
               RETURNING status-code
```

Parameters:

source	Any data item.
target	Any data item.
length	Numeric literal or PIC X(4) COMP-5.
status-code	See the section *Key*.

Description:

The routine starts at the left-hand end of source and target and ANDs the bits together, storing the result in target. The truth table for this is:

source	target	result
0	0	0
0	1	0
1	0	0
1	1	1

Parameters on Entry:

source	One of the data items to AND.
target	The other data item to AND.
length	The number of bytes of source and target to AND. Positions in target beyond this are unchanged.

Parameters on Exit:

target	The result.

CBL_CHANGE_DIR

Changes the current directory.

Syntax:

```
CALL "CBL_CHANGE_DIR" USING path-name
                      RETURNING status-code
```

Parameters:

path-name	PIC X(n).
status-code	See the section *Key*.

Parameters on Entry:

path-name	Relative or absolute path-name terminated by space or null (x"00"). This must be no longer than the number of characters allowed by your operating system and must be valid from the directory that is current when the routine is called.

Parameters on Exit:

None

CBL_CHECK_FILE_EXIST

Checks whether a file exists and returns details if it does.

Syntax:

```
CALL "CBL_CHECK_FILE_EXIST" USING file-name
                                  file-details
                           RETURNING status-code
```

Parameters:

file-name	PIC X(n).
file-details	Group item defined as:
file-size	PIC X(8) COMP-X.
file-date	
day	PIC X COMP-X.
month	PIC X COMP-X.
year	PIC X(2) COMP-X.
file-time	
hours	PIC X COMP-X.
minutes	PIC X COMP-X.
seconds	PIC X COMP-X.
hundredths	PIC X COMP-X.
status-code	See the section *Key*.

Parameters on Entry:

file-name   The file to look for. The name can contain a path-name, and is terminated by a space. If no path is given, the current directory is assumed.

Parameters on Exit:

file-size	The size of the file in bytes.
file-date	The date the file was created.
file-time	The time the file was created.

CBL_CLEAR_SCR

Clears the whole screen to a specified character and attribute.

Syntax:

```
CALL "CBL_CLEAR_SCR" USING character
                           attribute
                     RETURNING status-code
```

Parameters:

character	PIC X.
attribute	PIC X.
status-code	See the section *Key*.

Parameters on Entry:

character	The character to write.
attribute	The attribute to write.

Parameters on Exit:

None

CBL_CLOSE_FILE

Closes a file opened for byte-stream operations.

Syntax:

```
CALL "CBL_CLOSE_FILE" USING file-handle
                      RETURNING status-code
```

Parameters:

file-handle	PIC X(4).
status-code	See the section *Key*.

Description:

Any byte-stream file open when a STOP RUN is executed is automatically closed.

Parameters on Entry:

file-handle   The file handle returned when the file was opened.

Parameters on Exit:

None

CBL_CREATE_DIR

Creates a subdirectory. All the directories in the given path, except the last, must already exist.

Syntax:

```
CALL "CBL_CREATE_DIR" USING path-name
                      RETURNING status-code
```

Parameters:

path-name	PIC X(n).
status-code	See the section *Key*.

Parameters on Entry:

path-name	Relative or absolute path-name terminated by space or null (x"00").

Parameters on Exit:

None

CBL_CREATE_FILE

Creates a new file for byte-stream operations.

Syntax:

```
CALL "CBL_CREATE_FILE" USING file-name
                             access-mode
                             deny-mode
                             device
                             file-handle
                       RETURNING status-code
```

Parameters:

file-name	PIC X(n).
access-mode	PIC X COMP-X.
deny-mode	PIC X COMP-X.
device	PIC X COMP-X.
file-handle	PIC X(4).
status-code	See the section *Key*.

Parameters on Entry:

file-name	Space- or null-terminated file-name of the file to be opened.
access-mode	Defines access mode: 1= read only 2= write only (deny-mode must be 0) 3= read/write
deny-mode	Defines deny mode: Controls access to the file by other programs. 0= deny both read and write (exclusive) 1= deny write 2= deny read 3= deny neither read nor write
device	Reserved for future use (must be 0)

Parameters on Exit:

file-handle	Returns a file handle for a successful open.

CBL_DELETE_DIR

Deletes a directory. A directory will only be deleted if it is empty.

Syntax:

```
CALL "CBL_DELETE_DIR" USING path-name
                      RETURNING status-code
```

Parameters:

path-name	PIC X(n).
status-code	See the section *Key*.

Parameters on Entry:

path-name	Relative or absolute path-name terminated by space or null (x"00").

Parameters on Exit:

None

CBL_DELETE_FILE

Deletes a file

Syntax:

```
CALL "CBL_DELETE_FILE" USING file-name
                       RETURNING status-code
```

Parameters:

file-name	PIC X(n).
status-code	See the section *Key*.

Parameters on Entry:

file-name   The file to delete. The name can contain a path-name, and is terminated by a space. If no path is given, the current directory is assumed.

Parameters on Exit:

None

CBL_EQ

Does a logical EQUIVALENCE between the bits of two data items.

Syntax:

```
CALL "CBL_EQ" USING source
                    target
              BY VALUE length
              RETURNING status-code
```

Parameters:

source	Any data item.
target	Any data item
length	Numeric literal or PIC X(4) COMP-5.
status-code	See the section *Key*.

Description:

The routine starts at the left-hand end of source and target and EQUIVALENCEs the bits together, storing the result in target. The truth table for this is:

source	target	result
0	0	1
0	1	0
1	0	0
1	1	1

Parameters on Entry:

source	One of the data items to EQUIVALENCE.
target	The other data item to EQUIVALENCE.
length	The number of bytes of source and target to EQUIVALENCE. Positions in target beyond this length are unchanged.

Library Routines

Parameters on Exit:

target   The result.

CBL_GET_CSR_POS

Returns the cursor position.

Syntax:

```
CALL "CBL_GET_CSR_POS" USING screen-position
                       RETURNING status-code
```

Parameters:

screen-position   Group item defined as:
    row-number   PIC X COMP-X.
    column-number   PIC X COMP-X.
status-code   See the section *Key*.

Parameters on Entry:

None

Parameters on Exit:

screen-position   The screen position of the cursor. The top left
                           corner is row 0, column 0. If the cursor is
                           invisible, row-number and column-number
                           are both set to 255.

CBL_GET_KBD_STATUS

Checks whether there is a character waiting to be read from the keyboard.

Syntax:

```
CALL "CBL_GET_KBD_STATUS" USING key-status
                          RETURNING status-code
```

Parameters:

key-status   PIC X COMP-X.
status-code   See the section *Key*.

Parameters on Entry:

None

Parameters on Exit:

key-status   0 = no character available
                    1 = character available

CBL_GET_MOUSE_MASK

Returns the mouse event mask.

Syntax:

```
CALL "CBL_GET_MOUSE_MASK" USING mouse-handle
                                event-mask
                          RETURNING status-code
```

Parameters:

mouse-handle   PIC X(4) COMP-X.
event-mask   PIC X(2) COMP-X.
status-code   See the section *Key*.

Description:

See *Mouse* in *Routines by Category* earlier in this section.

Parameters on Entry:

mouse-handle	Mouse identifier, obtained by earlier call to CBL_INIT_MOUSE.

Parameters on Exit:

event-mask	See *Mouse* in the section *Routines by Category* earlier in this section.

CBL_GET_MOUSE_POSITION

Returns the screen position of the mouse pointer.

Syntax:

```
CALL "CBL_GET_MOUSE_POSITION" USING mouse-handle
                                    mouse-position
                             RETURNING status-code
```

Parameters:

mouse-handle	PIC X(4) COMP-X.
mouse-position	Group item defined as:
mouse-row	PIC X(2) COMP-X.
mouse-col	PIC X(2) COMP-X.
status-code	See the section *Key*.

Description:

See *Mouse* in *Routines by Category* earlier in this section.

Parameters on Entry:

mouse-handle   Mouse identifier, obtained by earlier call to
                      CBL_INIT_MOUSE.

Parameters on Exit:

mouse-position   The screen position of the mouse pointer.

CBL_GET_MOUSE_STATUS

Finds out the number of events in the queue.

Syntax:

```
CALL "CBL_GET_MOUSE_STATUS" USING mouse-handle
                                  queued-events
                           RETURNING status-code
```

Parameters:

mouse-handle   PIC X(4) COMP-X.
queued-events   PIC X(2) COMP-X.
status-code   See the section *Key*.

Description:

See *Mouse* in *Routines by Category* earlier in this section.

Parameters on Entry:

mouse-handle   Mouse identifier, obtained by earlier call to
                      CBL_INIT_MOUSE.

Parameters on Exit:

    queued-events   The number of events in the queue.

CBL_GET_SCR_SIZE

Returns information on the size of the screen.

Syntax:

```
CALL "CBL_GET_SCR_SIZE" USING depth
                              width
                        RETURNING status-code
```

Parameters:

depth	PIC X COMP-X.
width	PIC X COMP-X.
status-code	See the section *Key*.

Parameters on Entry:

    None

Parameters on Exit:

depth	Number of lines.
width	Number of columns.

CBL_HIDE_MOUSE

Makes the mouse pointer invisible.

Syntax:

```
CALL "CBL_HIDE_MOUSE" USING mouse-handle
                      RETURNING status-code
```

Parameters:

mouse-handle	PIC X(4) COMP-X
status-code	See the section *Key*.

Description:

After this routine has been called, mouse events still take place, but the mouse pointer is not displayed.

See also *Mouse* in *Routines by Category* earlier in this section.

Parameters on Entry:

mouse-handle	Mouse identifier, obtained by earlier call to CBL_INIT_MOUSE.

Parameters on Exit:

None

CBL_IMP

Does a logical IMPLIES between the bits of two data items.

Syntax:

```
CALL "CBL_IMP" USING source
                     target
               BY VALUE length
               RETURNING status-code
```

Parameters:

source	Any data item.
target	Any data item.
length	Numeric literal or PIC X(4) COMP-5.
status-code	See the section *Key*.

Description:

The routine starts at the left-hand end of source and target and IMPLIES the bits together, storing the result in target. The truth table for this is:

source	target	result
0	0	1
0	1	1
1	0	0
1	1	1

Parameters on Entry:

source	One of the data items to IMPLIES.
target	The other data item to IMPLIES.
length	The number of bytes of source and target to IMPLIES. Positions in target beyond this are unchanged.

Parameters on Exit:

target   The result.

CBL_INIT_MOUSE

Initializes mouse support. This routine must be called before other mouse routines can be called.

Syntax:

```
CALL "CBL_INIT_MOUSE" USING mouse-handle
                            mouse-buttons
                      RETURNING status-code
```

Parameters:

mouse-handle   PIC X(4) COMP-X
mouse-buttons   PIC X(2) COMP-X
status-code   See the section *Key*.

Description:

See Mouse in *Routines by Category* earlier in this section.

Parameters on Entry:

None

Parameters on Exit:

mouse-handle   Mouse identifier. You pass this to any mouse routines you call subsequently.

mouse-buttons   The number of buttons on the mouse.

CBL_JOIN_FILENAME

Forms a file-name by joining together its component parts; that is, the device-name, base-name path and extension.

Syntax:

```
CALL "CBL_JOIN_FILENAME" USING split-join-params
                               join-buffer
                               device-buffer
                               basename-buffer
                               extension-buffer
                         RETURNING status-code
```

Parameters:

split-join-params	Group item defined as:
param-length	PIC X(2) COMP-X.
split-join-flag1	PIC X COMP-X.
split-join-flag2	PIC X COMP-X.
device-offset	PIC X(2) COMP-X.
device-length	PIC X(2) COMP-X.
basename-offset	PIC X(2) COMP-X.
basename-length	PIC X(2) COMP-X
extension-offset	PIC X(2) COMP-X.
extension-length	PIC X(2) COMP-X
total-length	PIC X(2) COMP-X.
split-buf-len	PIC X(2) COMP-X.
join-buf-len	PIC X(2) COMP-X.
first-path-component-length	PIC X(2) COMP-X.
join-buffer	PIC X(n).
device-buffer	PIC X(n)
basename-buffer	PIC X(n).
extension-buffer	PIC X(n).
status-code	See the section *Key*.

Description:

The new file-name is formed by concatenating:

■ the first *device-length* bytes (starting from device-offset) of *device-buffer*

■ the first *basename-length* bytes (starting from basename-offset) of *basename-buffer*

■ the first *extension-length* bytes (starting from extension-offset) of *extension-buffer*

and is placed in *join-buffer* with length *total-length*.

This routine can be made to fold to upper case by setting the least significant bit (bit 0) of *split-join-flag1*. If this bit is not set, the case will be preserved.

This routine can accept either null-terminated or space-terminated strings. Setting the second least significant bit (bit 1) of *split-join-flag1* results in the routine expecting null-terminated strings. If this bit is not set, space-terminated strings are expected.

The device, base-name, and extension fields can be shorter than the lengths specified by *device-length*, *basename-length*, and *extension-length* respectively, if they are terminated with either a space or a null, depending on the setting of bit 1 of *split-join-flag1*.

device-buffer, *basename-buffer*, *extension-buffer*, and *join-buffer* do not have to be four distinct buffers. This means that this routine can be used with CBL_SPLIT_FILENAME to replace one component of a file-name.

If *device-buffer* is not empty and does not have a trailing "\" or "/" or colon, and *basename-buffer* is not empty, the routine inserts a "\" between the device and base-name in *join-buffer*.

If extension is ".", the string returned in *join-buffer* has an extension of spaces; that is, the file-name has a trailing dot.

If *total-length* is less than *join-buf-len*, the characters after the end of the file-name are nulls or spaces depending on bit 1 of *split-join-flag1*.

If device consists of a valid drive letter, but no colon, the routine adds one. It does not do this for a device (for example, LPT1) that does not need one. You cannot join a device (for example, LPT1, as opposed to a drive letter) to a non-empty base-name.

See also *File-names* in *Routines by Category* earlier in this section and the description of CBL_SPLIT_FILENAME.

Parameters on Entry:

param-length	Length of *split-join-params* in bytes, including the two bytes for *param-length*. The normal value for *param-length* is 24.
split-join-flag1	bit 1 - if set, specifies that the strings are null-terminated, otherwise they are space-terminated.
	bit 0 - if set, specifies that the new file-name will be folded to upper case, otherwise the original case will be preserved.
device-offset	Offset of the start of the device in *device-buffer* (indexed from one).
device-length	Length of device if not space- or null-terminated.
basename-offset	Offset of the start of the basename in *basename-buffer* (indexed from one).
basename-length	Length of base-name if not space- or null-terminated.
extension-offset	Offset of the start of the extension in *extension-buffer* (indexed from one).
extension-length	Length of extension if not space- or null-terminated.
device-buffer	Device-name.
basename-buffer	Base-name.

extension-buffer	Extension.
join-buf-len	Length of join-buffer.

Parameters on Exit:

total-length	Total number of characters in the file-name.
join-buffer	The joined-up file-name.
status-code	Return status:
	0 = success
	1 = file-name too big for *join-buffer*
	4 = illegal file-name

CBL_NOT

Does a logical NOT on the bits of a data item

Syntax:

```
CALL "CBL_NOT" USING target
               BY VALUE length
               RETURNING status-code
```

Parameters:

target	Any data item.
length	Numeric literal or PIC X(4) COMP-5.
status-code	See the section *Key*.

Description:

The routine starts at the left-hand end of target and inverts bits. The truth table for this is:

before	after
0	1
1	0

See also *Logic Operators* in *Routines by Category* earlier in this section.

Parameters on Entry:

target   The data to operate on.

Parameters on Exit:

target   The data with the bits inverted.
length   The number of bytes of target to change. Positions beyond this are unchanged.

CBL_OPEN_FILE

Opens an existing file for byte-stream operations.

Syntax:

```
CALL "CBL_OPEN_FILE" USING file-name
                           access-mode
                           deny-mode
                           device
                           file-handle
                     RETURNING status-code
```

Parameters:

file-name   PIC X(n).
access-mode   PIC X COMP-X
deny-mode   PIC X COMP-X.
device   PIC X COMP-X.
file-handle   PIC X(4).status-code
status-code   See the section *Key*.

Description:

See *Byte-stream Files* in *Routines by Category* earlier in this section.

Parameters on Entry:

file-name	Space- or null-terminated file-name of the file to be opened.
access-mode	Defines access mode: 1 = read only 2 = write only (deny-mode must be 0) 3 = read/write
deny-mode	Defines deny mode: controls access to the file by other programs. 0 = deny both read and write (exclusive) 1 = deny write 2 = deny read 3 = deny neither read nor write
device	Reserved for future use (must be 0).

Parameters on Exit:

file-handle	Returns a file handle for a successful open.

CBL_OR

Does a logical OR between the bits of two data items.

Syntax:

```
CALL "CBL_OR" USING source
                    target
              BY VALUE length
              RETURNING status-code
```

Parameters:

source	Any data item.
target	Any data item.
length	Numeric literal or PIC X(4) COMP-5.
status-code	See the section *Key*.

Description:

The routine starts at the left-hand end of source and target and ORs the bits together, storing the result in target. The truth table for this is:

source	target	result
0	0	0
0	1	1
1	0	1
1	1	1

See also *Logic Operators* in *Routines by Category* earlier in this section.

Parameters on Entry:

source	One of the data items to OR.
target	The other data item to OR.
length	The number of bytes of source and target to OR.Positions in target beyond this are unchanged.

Parameters on Exit:

target	The result.

CBL_READ_DIR

Returns the current directory or path.

Syntax:

```
CALL "CBL_READ_DIR" USING path-name
                          path-name-length
                    RETURNING status-code
```

Parameters:

path-name	PIC X(n).
path-name-length	PIC X COMP-X.
status-code	See the section *Key*.

Parameters on Entry:

path-name-length	Length of path-name to be used. If this is too small for the path-name, the routine fails.

Parameters on Exit:

path-name	Relative or absolute path-name terminated by space or null (x"00").

CBL_READ_FILE

Reads bytes from a file.

Syntax:

```
CALL "CBL_READ_FILE" USING file-handle
                           file-offset
                           byte-count
                           flags
                           buffer
                     RETURNING status-code
```

Parameters:

file-handle	PIC X(4).
file-offset	PIC X(8) COMP-X.
byte-count	PIC X(4) COMP-X.
flags	PIC X COMP-X.
buffer	PIC X(n)
status-code	See the section *Key*.

Description:

See also *Byte-Stream Files* in *Routines by Category* earlier in this section.

Parameters on Entry:

file-handle	The file handle returned when the file was opened.
file-offset	The offset in file at which to read. This field is currently limited to a maximum value of x"00FFFFFFFF".
byte-count	The number of bytes to read. This field is currently limited to a maximum value of x"00FFFF".
flags	This parameter can take the following values: 0 = for standard read 128 = to have the current file size returned in the *file-offset* field

Parameters on Exit:

file-offset	Contains the current file size on return if the flags parameter is set to 128 on entry.
buffer	The buffer into which the bytes are read. It is your responsibility to ensure that the buffer is large enough to hold the number of bytes to be read. The buffer parameter is allowed to cross a 64K segment boundary.

CBL_READ_KBD_CHAR

Waits until a character is typed and then reads it with no echo.

Syntax:

```
CALL "CBL_READ_KBD_CHAR" USING char
                         RETURNING status-code
```

Parameters:

char	PIC X.
status-code	See the section *Key*.

Parameters on Entry:

None

Parameters on Exit:

char   The character that was typed, in ASCII.

CBL_READ_MOUSE_EVENT

Reads the mouse event queue and returns information about an event.

Syntax:

```
CALL "CBL_READ_MOUSE_EVENT" USING mouse-handle
                                  event-data
                                  read-type
                           RETURNING status-code
```

Parameters:

mouse-handle   PIC X(4) COMP-X.

event-data   See *Mouse* in *Routines by Category* earlier in this section.

read-type   PIC X COMP-X.

status-code   See the section *Key*.

Description:

If there are no events in the event queue, the return from this routine depends on the value of *read-type*. If *read-type* is zero, the routine returns immediately with all zero values in *event-data*. If *read-type* has a value of one, return is delayed until an event has been queued.

See also *Mouse* in *Routines by Category* earlier in this section.

Parameters on Entry:

mouse-handle	Mouse identifier, obtained by earlier call to CBL_INIT_MOUSE.
read-type	Indicates what to do if there are no events in the queue: 0 = return immediately 1 = wait for an event, then return.

Parameters on Exit:

event-data	See *Mouse* in *Routines by Category* earlier in this section.

CBL_READ_SCR_ATTRS

Reads a string of attributes from the screen.

Syntax:

```
CALL "CBL_READ_SCR_ATTRS" USING screen-position
                                 attribute-buffer
                                 string-length
                          RETURNING status-code
```

Parameters:

screen-position	Group item defined as:
row-number	PIC X COMP-X.
column-number	PIC X COMP-X.
attribute-buffer	PIC X(n).
string-length	PIC X(2) COMP-X.
status-code	See the section *Key*.

Parameters on Entry:

screen-position	The screen position to start reading at. The top left corner is row 0, column 0.
string-length	The length of the string to read.

Parameters on Exit

attribute-buffer	The attributes read from the screen. This data item must be at least as long as specified by string-length; positions in it beyond that length are unchanged.
string-length	If the end of the screen is reached, the length read is returned in here.

CBL_READ_SCR_CHARS

Reads a string of characters from the screen.

Syntax:

```
CALL "CBL_READ_SCR_CHARS" USING screen-position
                                character-buffer
                                string-length
                          RETURNING status-code
```

Library Routines

Parameters:

screen-position	Group item defined as:
row-number	PIC X COMP-X
column-number	PIC X COMP-X.
character-buffer	PIC X(n).
string-length	PIC X(2) COMP-X.
status-code	See the section *Key*.

Parameters on Entry:

screen-position	The screen position at which to start reading. The top left corner is row 0, column 0.
string-length	The length of the string to read.

Parameters on Exit:

character-buffer	The characters read from the screen. This data item must be at least as long as specified by *string-length*; positions in it beyond that length are unchanged.
string-length	If the end of the screen is reached, the length read is returned in here.

CBL_READ_SCR_CHATTRS

Reads a string of characters and their attributes from the screen.

Syntax:

```
CALL "CBL_READ_SCR_CHATTRS" USING screen-position
                                  character-buffer
                                  attribute-buffer
                                  string-length
                           RETURNING status-code
```

Parameters:

screen-position	Group item defined as:
row-number	PIC X COMP-X.
column-number	PIC X COMP-X.
character-buffer	PIC X(n).
attribute-buffer	PIC X(n).
string-length	PIC X(2) COMP-X.
status-code	See the section *Key*.

Parameters on Entry:

screen-position	The screen position at which to start reading.The top left corner is row 0, column 0.
string-length	The length of the string to read.

Parameters on Exit:

character-buffer	The characters read from the screen. This data item must be at least as long as specified by *string-length*; positions in it beyond that length are unchanged.
attribute-buffer	The attributes read from the screen. This data item must be at least as long as specified by *string-length*; positions in it beyond that length are unchanged.
string-length	If the end of the screen is reached, the length read (in cells, that is, character-attribute pairs) is returned in here.

CBL_RENAME_FILE

Changes the name of a file.

Syntax:

```
CALL "CBL_RENAME_FILE" USING old-file-name
                             new-file-name
                       RETURNING status-code
```

Parameters:

old-file-name	PIC X(n)
new-file-name	PIC X(n).
status-code	See the section *Key*.

Parameters on Entry:

old-file-name
: The file to rename. The name can contain a *path-name*, and is terminated by a space. If no path is given, the current directory is assumed.

new-file-name
: The new name, terminated by a space. If old-file-name contains a path-name, this must contain the same path-name.

Parameters on Exit:

None

CBL_SET_CSR_POS

Moves the curso.r

Syntax:

```
CALL "CBL_SET_CSR_POS" USING screen-position
                       RETURNING status-code
```

Parameters:

screen-position	Group item defined as:
row-number	PIC X COMP-X.
column-number	PIC X COMP-X.
status-code	See the section *Key*.

Parameters on Entry:

screen-position   The screen position at which to put the cursor. The top left corner is row 0, column 0. To make the cursor invisible, set row-number and column-number to 255. Any other legal on-screen values make the cursor visible.

Parameters on Exit:

None

CBL_SET_MOUSE_MASK

Sets the mouse event mask.

Syntax:

```
CALL "CBL_SET_MOUSE_MASK" USING mouse-handle
                                event-mask
                          RETURNING status-code
```

Parameters:

mouse-handle	PIC X(4) COMP-X.
event-mask	PIC X(2) COMP-X.
status-code	See the section *Key*.

Description:

CBL_GET_MOUSE_MASK should be called first to find out which events are enabled.

See also *Mouse* in *Routines by Category* earlier in this section.

Parameters on Entry:

mouse-handle	Mouse identifier, obtained by earlier call to CBL_INIT_MOUSE.
event-mask	See *Mouse* in *Routines by Category* earlier in this section.

Parameters on Exit:

None

CBL_SET_MOUSE_POSITION

Moves the mouse pointer.

Syntax:

```
CALL "CBL_SET_MOUSE_POSITION" USING mouse-handle
                                   mouse-position
                            RETURNING status-code
```

Parameters:

mouse-handle	PIC X(4) COMP-X.
mouse-position	Group item defined as:
mouse-row	PIC X(2) COMP-X.
mouse-col	PIC X(2) COMP-X.
status-code	See the section *Key*.

Description:

See *Mouse* in *Routines by Category* earlier in this section.

Parameters on Entry:

mouse-handle   Mouse identifier, obtained by earlier call to CBL_INIT_MOUSE.

mouse-position   The screen position to move the mouse pointer to.

Parameters on Exit:

None

CBL_SHOW_MOUSE

Makes the mouse pointer visible.

Syntax:

```
CALL "CBL_SHOW_MOUSE" USING mouse-handle
                      RETURNING status-code
```

Parameters:

mouse-handle   PIC X(4) COMP-X
status-code   See the section *Key*.

Description:

When the mouse support has been initialized by the CBL_INIT_MOUSE call, the pointer is not displayed until this routine is called. After this call the system displays the mouse pointer until a routine to hide the mouse or terminate mouse support is called. This routine cancels any collision area defined earlier by PC_SET_MOUSE_HIDE_AREA.

See also *Mouse* in *Routines by Category* earlier in this section.

Parameters on Entry:

mouse-handle	Mouse identifier, obtained by earlier call to CBL_INIT_MOUSE.

Parameters on Exit:

None

CBL_SPLIT_FILENAME

Splits a file-name into its component parts; that is, the device-name, base-name and extension.

Syntax:

```
CALL "CBL_SPLIT_FILENAME" USING  split-join-params
                                 split-buffer
                          RETURNING status-code
```

Parameters:

split-join-params	Group item defined as:
param-length	PIC X(2) COMP-X.
split-join-flag1	PIC X COMP-X.
split-join-flag2	PIC X COMP-X.
device-offset	PIC X(2) COMP-X
device-length	PIC X(2) COMP-X.
basename-offset	PIC X(2) COMP-X.
basename-length	PIC X(2) COMP-X.
extension-offset	PIC X(2) COMP-X.
extension-length	PIC X(2) COMP-X.
total-length	PIC X(2) COMP-X.
split-buf-len	PIC X(2) COMP-X.
join-buf-len	PIC X(2) COMP-X.
first-path-component-length	PIC X(2) COMP-X.
split-buffer	PIC X(n)
status-code	See the section *Key*.

Description:

This routine can be made to fold to upper case by setting the least significant bit (bit 0) of *split-join-flag1*. If this bit is not set, the case will be preserved.

This routine can accept either null-terminated or space-terminated strings. Setting the second least significant bit (bit 1) of *split-join-flag1* results in the routine expecting null-terminated strings. If this bit is not set, space-terminated strings are expected.

If there are two or more dots in the file-name (not counting dots in the device or *path-name*), the extension returned consists of the characters between the last dot and the end of the file-name. The base-name contains everything up to, but not including, the last dot.

To make a distinction between file-names with no extension and file-names with spaces extension (that is, base-names whose last character is a dot), if the extension is spaces *extension-length* is 1 and *extension-offset* points to the last dot.

See also *File-names* in *Routines by Category* earlier in this section and the description for CBL_JOIN_FILENAME.

Parameters on Entry:

param-length	Length of *split-join-params* in bytes, including the two bytes for *param-length*. The normal value for *param-length* is 24.
split-join-flag1	bit 1 - if set, specifies that the file-name is null-terminated, otherwise it is space-terminated. bit 0 - if set, specifies that the new strings will be folded to upper case, otherwise the original case will be preserved.
split-buf-len	Length of *split-buffer*.
split-buffer	The string to split.

Library Routines

Parameters on Exit:

split-join-flag2	bit 1 - set if there is a wildcard in the device. bit 0 - set if there is a wildcard in base-name or extension.
device-offset	Start of device-name in *split-buffer*, from one.
device-length	Length of *device-name*; zero if there is none. This includes any following colon.
basename-offset	Start of *base-name* in split-buffer, from one.
basename-length	Length of *base-name*; zero if there is none. This does not include the following dot.
extension-offset	Start of extension in *split-buffer*, from one.
extension-length	Length of extension; zero if there is none. This does not include the preceding dot.
total-length	Total number of characters in the string.
first-path-component-length	Number of characters up to and including the first \ or / or colon; if *split-buffer* contains none of these, this field = *device-length*.
split-buffer	Unchanged unless bit 1 of *split-join-flag1* is set, when it is folded to upper case.
status-code	0 = success 4 = illegal file-name

CBL_SWAP_SCR_CHATTRS

Swaps a string of characters and their attributes with a string from the screen.

Syntax:

```
CALL "CBL_SWAP_SCR_CHATTRS" USING screen-position
                                  character-buffer
                                  attribute-buffer
                                  string-length
                            RETURNING status-code
```

Parameters:

screen-position	Group item defined as:
row-number	PIC X COMP-X.
column-number	PIC X COMP-X.
character-buffer	PIC X(n).
attribute-buffer	PIC X(n).
string-length	PIC X(2) COMP-X.
status-code	See the section *Key*.

Parameters on Entry:

screen-position	The screen position at which to start writing. The top left corner is row 0, column 0.
character-buffer	The characters to write.
attribute-buffer	The attributes to write.
string-length	The length of the string to write. If this would go off the end of the screen, the write finishes at the end of the screen.

Parameters on Exit:

character-buffer	The characters read from the screen. This *data item* must be at least as long as specified by *string-length*; positions in it beyond that length are unchanged.
attribute-buffer	The attributes read from the screen. This *data item* must be at least as long as specified by *string-length*; positions in it beyond that length are unchanged.
string-length	If the end of the screen is reached the length swapped (in cells, that is, character-attribute pairs) is returned in here.

CBL_TERM_MOUSE

Terminates mouse support, releasing internal resources.

Syntax:

```
CALL "CBL_TERM_MOUSE" USING mouse-handle
                      RETURNING status-code
```

Parameters:

mouse-handle	PIC X(4) COMP-X
status-code	See the section *Key*.

Description:

The routine releases internal resources allocated by
CBL_INIT_MOUSE. After this routine, mouse-handle is no longer
valid and calling any mouse routine other than
CBL_INIT_MOUSE will result in an error.

See also *Mouse* in *Routines by Category* earlier in this section.

Parameters on Entry:

mouse-handle	Mouse identifier, obtained by earlier call to CBL_INIT_MOUSE.

Parameters on Exit:

None

CBL_TOLOWER

Converts a string of letters to lower case.

Syntax:

```
CALL "CBL_TOLOWER" USING string
                   BY VALUE length
                   RETURNING status-code
```

Parameters:

string	PIC X(n).
length	PIC X(4)COMP-5
status-code	See the section *Key*.

Description:

The routine starts at the left-hand end of string and converts letters to lower case (also called folding to lower case).

Parameters on Entry:

string	The string to convert
length	The number of bytes of string to change; positions beyond this are unchanged.

Parameters on Exit:

string	The converted string.

CBL_TOUPPER

Converts a string of letters to upper case.

Syntax:

```
CALL "CBL_TOUPPER" USING string
                   BY VALUE length
                   RETURNING status-code
```

Parameters:

string	PIC X(n)
length	PIC X(4) COMP-5.
status-code	See the section *Key*.

Description:

The routine starts at the left-hand end of string and converts letters to upper case (also called folding to upper case).

Parameters on Entry:

string	The string to convert.
length	The number of bytes of string to change; positions beyond this are unchanged.

Parameters on Exit:

string	The converted string.

CBL_WRITE_FILE

Writes bytes to a file.

Syntax:

```
CALL "CBL_WRITE_FILE" USING file-handle
                            file-offset
                            byte-count
                            flags
                            buffer
                      RETURNING status-code
```

Parameters:

file-handle	PIC X(4).
file-offset	PIC X(8) COMP-X.
byte-count	PIC X(4) COMP-X.
flags	PIC X COMP-X.
buffer	PIC X(n).
status-code	See the section *Key*.

Description:

See *Byte-stream Files* in *Routines by Category* earlier in this section.

Parameters on Entry:

file-handle	The file handle returned when the file was opened.
file-offset	The offset in file at which to write. This field is currently limited to a maximum value of x"00FFFFFFFF".
byte-count	The number of bytes to write. This field is currently limited to a maximum value of x"00FFFF". Putting a value of zero in this field will cause the file to be truncated or extended to the size specified in the file-offset field.

flags   This parameter can take the following value:
0 = for standard write

buffer   The buffer from which the bytes are written. It is your responsibility to ensure that the buffer is large enough to hold the number of bytes to be written.
The buffer parameter is allowed to cross a 64 Kilobyte segment boundary.

Parameters on Exit:

None

CBL_WRITE_SCR_ATTRS

Writes a string of attributes to the screen.

Syntax:

```
CALL "CBL_WRITE_SCR_ATTRS" USING screen-position
                                 attribute-buffer
                                 string-length
                      RETURNING status-code
```

Parameters:

screen-position	Group item defined as:
row-number	PIC X COMP-X.
column-number	PIC X COMP-X.
attribute-buffer	PIC X(n).
string-length	PIC X(2) COMP-X.
status-code	See the section *Key*.

Parameters on Entry:

screen-position   The screen position at which to start writing. The top left corner is row 0, column 0.

attribute-buffer	The attributes to write.
string-length	The length of the string to write. If this would go off the end of the screen, the write finishes at the end of the screen.

Parameters on Exit:

None

CBL_WRITE_SCR_CHARS

Writes a string of characters to the screen.

Syntax:

```
CALL "CBL_WRITE_SCR_CHARS" USING screen-position
                                 character-buffer
                                 string-length
                          RETURNING status-code
```

Parameters:

screen-position	Group item defined as:
row-number	PIC X COMP-X
column-number	PIC X COMP-X.
character-buffer	PIC X(n).
string-length	PIC X(2) COMP-X.
status-code	See the section *Key*.

Parameters on Entry:

screen-position	The screen position at which to start writing. The top left corner is row 0, column 0.
character-buffer	The characters to write.
string-length	The length of the string to write. If this would go off the end of the screen, the write finishes at the end of the screen.

Library Routines

Parameters on Exit:

None

CBL_WRITE_SCR_CHARS_ATTR

Writes a string of characters to the screen, giving them all the same attribute.

Syntax:

```
CALL "CBL_WRITE_SCR_CHARS_ATTR" USING screen-position
                                      character-buffer
                                      string-length
                                      attribute
                               RETURNING status-code
```

Parameters:

screen-position	Group item defined as:
row-number	PIC X COMP-X.
column-number	PIC X COMP-X.
character-buffer	PIC X(n).
attribute	PIC X.
string-length	PIC X(2) COMP-X.
status-code	See the section *Key*.

Parameters on Entry:

screen-position	The screen position at which to start writing. The top left corner is row 0, column 0.
character-buffer	The characters to write.
attribute	The attribute to write.
string-length	The length of the string to write.

Parameters on Exit:

None

CBL_WRITE_SCR_CHATTRS

Writes a string of characters and their attributes to the screen.

Syntax:

```
CALL "CBL_WRITE_SCR_CHATTRS" USING screen-position
                                   character-buffer
                                   attribute-buffer
                                   string-length
                             RETURNING status-code
```

Parameters:

screen-position	Group item defined as:
row-number	PIC X COMP-X.
column-number	PIC X COMP-X.
character-buffer	PIC X(n).
attribute-buffer	PIC X(n).
string-length	PIC X(2) COMP-X.
status-code	See the section *Key*.

Parameters on Entry:

screen-position	The screen position at which to start writing. The top left corner is row 0, column 0.
character-buffer	The characters to write.
attribute-buffer	The attributes to write.
string-length	The length of the string to write. If this would go off the end of the screen, the write finishes at the end of the screen.

Parameters on Exit:

None

CBL_WRITE_SCR_N_ATTR

Writes a specified attribute to a string of positions on the screen.

Syntax:

```
CALL "CBL_WRITE_SCR_N_ATTR" USING screen-position
                                  attribute
                                  fill-length
                           RETURNING status-code
```

Parameters:

screen-position	Group item defined as:
row-number	PIC X COMP-X.
column-number	PIC X COMP-X.
attribute	PIC X.
fill-length	PIC X(2) COMP-X.
status-code	See the section *Key*.

Parameters on Entry:

screen-position	The screen position at which to start writing. The top left corner is row 0, column 0.
attribute	The attribute to write.
string-length	The number of screen positions to write the attribute to. If this would go off the end of the screen, the write finishes at the end of the screen.

Parameters on Exit:

None

CBL_WRITE_SCR_N_CHAR

Writes a specified character to a string of positions on the screen.

Syntax:

```
CALL "CBL_WRITE_SCR_N_CHAR" USING screen-position
                                  character
                                  fill-length
                           RETURNING status-code
```

Parameters:

screen-position	Group item defined as:
row-number	PIC X COMP-X.
column-number	PIC X COMP-X.
character	PIC X.
fill-length	PIC X(2) COMP-X.
status-code	See the section *Key*.

Parameters on Entry:

screen-position	The screen position at which to start writing. The top left corner is row 0, column 0.
character	The character to write.
string-length	The number of screen positions to write the character to. If this would go off the end of the screen, the write finishes at the end of the screen.

Parameters on Exit:

None

CBL_WRITE_SCR_N_CHATTR

Writes a specified character and attribute to a string of positions on the screen.

Syntax:

```
CALL "CBL_WRITE_SCR_N_CHATTR" USING screen-position
                                    character
                                    attribute
                                    fill-length
                             RETURNING status-code
```

Parameters:

screen-position	Group item defined as:
row-number	PIC X COMP-X
column-number	PIC X COMP-X.
character	PIC X.
attribute	PIC X.
fill-length	PIC X(2) COMP-X.
status-code	See the section *Key*.

Parameters on Entry:

screen-position	The screen position at which to start writing. The top left corner is row 0, column 0.
character	The character to write.
attribute	The attribute to write.
string-length	The number of screen positions to write the character-attribute pair to. If this would go off the end of the screen, the write finishes at the end of the screen.

Parameters on Exit:

None

CBL_WRITE_SCR_TTY

Writes a string of characters to the screen starting at the current position and scrolling.

Syntax:

```
CALL "CBL_WRITE_SCR_TTY" USING character-buffer
                               string-length
                         RETURNING status-code
```

Parameters:

character-buffer	IC X(n)
string-length	PIC X(2) COMP-X
status-code	See the section *Key*.

Parameters on Entry:

character-buffer	The characters to write.
string-length	The length of the string to write. If this goes off the edge of the screen, the screen is scrolled up a line and the write continues on the bottom line.

Parameters on Exit:

None

CBL_XOR

Does a logical XOR between the bits of two data items.

Syntax:

```
CALL "CBL_XOR" USING source
                     target
               BY VALUE length
               RETURNING status-code
```

Parameters:

source	Any data item.
target	Any data item.
length	Numeric literal or PIC X(4) COMP-5.
status-code	See the section *Key*.

Description:

The routine starts at the left-hand end of source and target and exclusive-ORs the bits together, storing the result in target. The truth table for this is:

source	target	result
0	0	0
0	1	1
1	0	1
1	1	0

See also *Logic Operators in Routines by Category* earlier in this section.

Parameters on Entry:

source	One of the data items to exclusive-OR.
target	The other data item to exclusive-OR.
length	The number of bytes of *source* and *target* to

exclusive-OR. Positions in *target* beyond this are unchanged.

Parameters on Exit:

target   The result.

PC_EXIT_PROC

Posts or removes a closedown procedure to be invoked automatically when the application terminates.

Syntax:

```
CALL "PC_EXIT_PROC" USING install-flag
                          install-address
                    RETURNING status-code
```

Parameters:

install-flag   PIC X COMP-X.
install-address   USAGE PROCEDURE-POINTER
status-code   See the section *Key*.

Description:

The routine sets RETURN-CODE to zero for success, nonzero for failure. The procedure will be executed whether the application finishes normally (with a STOP RUN) or abnormally (with a Ctrl+Brk, RTS error, etc). You can install several closedown procedures for an application by repeated calls of this routine.

A closedown procedure can be written in any language. If it is in COBOL, *install-address* must be the address of an entry point. You can obtain this address using the statement:

set *install-address* to entry *entry-name*

A closedown procedure in COBOL can include any legal COBOL, including CALL statements. The closedown procedure will terminate when the main program in the procedure does an EXIT PROGRAM/GOBACK or when a STOP RUN statement is executed.

A closedown procedure in any other language must preserve the i86 machine code BP register and direction flag, and terminate with a far return (RETF) instruction; that is, it must be a far procedure.

Parameters on Entry:

install-flag	Indicates the operation to be performed: 0 = install closedown procedure 1 = de-install closedown procedure
install-address	Address of closedown procedure.

Parameters on Exit:

None

PC_GET_MOUSE_SHAPE

Returns information about the shape of the mouse pointer.

Syntax:

```
CALL "PC_GET_MOUSE_SHAPE" USING mouse-handle
                                reserved-item
                                mouse-ptr-shape
                          RETURNING status-code
```

Parameters:

mouse-handle	PIC X(4) COMP-X.
reserved-item	PIC X(10).
mouse-ptr-shape	Group item defined as:

char_AND_mask	PIC X COMP-X.
attr_AND_mask	PIC X COMP-X.
char_XOR_mask	PIC X COMP-X.
attr_XOR_mask	PIC X COMP-X.
status-code	See the section *Key*.

Description:

The masks in *mouse-ptr-shape* are bit maps that, applied to a screen position, would superimpose the mouse shape upon it. The pointer shape is formed by PC_SET_MOUSE_SHAPE by ANDing the screen character at the mouse position with char_AND_mask, XORing the result with char_XOR_mask, and then displaying the result on the screen. The attribute is formed similarly.

To call this routine you must have previously called PC_SET_MOUSE_SHAPE with the same *mouse-handle*. The data item *reserved-item* must be as preserved from that call.

See also *Mouse* in *Routines by Category* earlier in this section.

Parameters on Entry:

mouse-handle	Mouse identifier, obtained by earlier call to CBL_INIT_MOUSE.
reserved-item	Reserved for future use.

Parameters on Exit:

mouse-ptr-shape	The bit maps that would create the pointer's current shape.

Library Routines

PC_LOCATE_FILE

This routine has two uses. It can be used to expand an environment variable in a file specification, where the environment variable contains a list of several paths. It can also determine whether an OPEN INPUT using a particular file specification will find the file in a library or as a separate disk file.

Syntax:

```
CALL "PC_LOCATE_FILE" USING user-file-spec
                            user-mode
                            actual-file-spec
                            exist-flag
                            path-flag
                      RETURNING status-code
```

Parameters:

user-file-spec	PIC X(n).
user-mode	PIC X COMP-X.
actual-file-spec	Group item defined as:
buffer-len	PIC X(2) COMP-X.
buffer	PIC X(n).
exist-flag	PIC X COMP-X.
path-flag	PIC X COMP-X.
status-code	See the section *Key*.

Parameters on Entry:

user-file-spec Contains the file-name specification; this can include an embedded environment variable or library name. For example:
standard file-name
  device\file-name.ext
embedded environment variable:
  $envname\file-name.ext
embedded library name:
  device\library-name.LBR\file-name.ext

user-mode Specifies what to do with *user-file-spec*:
0 = Check whether the file exists in a

library or as a separate disk file.

If *user-file-spec* includes an embedded library-name, that library is opened (if it exists)and searched for the file. The library is left open afterwards.

If *user-file-spec* includes an embedded environment variable, the file will be searched for along each path specified in that variable. If it is found, *actual-file-spec* on exit contains the file specification with the environment variable expanded to the successful path.

Otherwise, *actual-file-spec* on exit contains the file specification with the environment variable expanded to the first path it contained.

1 = If *user-file-spec* includes an environment variable, *actual-file-spec* on exit contains the file specification with the environment variable expanded to the first path it contained. The file is not searched for.

2 = If *user-file-spec* includes an environment variable, *actual-file-spec* on exit contains the file specification with the environment variable expanded to the next path it contained. The file is not searched for. This option should only be used after a successful call with *user-mode* = 1 or 2. See path-flag below.

path-flag   If *user-mode* = 2, this data item should contain the value that was returned in this item from the previous *user-mode* = 1 or 2 call.

Parameters on Exit:

buffer-len   Size of following buffer.
buffer   Buffer to contain the resolved file specification, as described under user-mode.

exist-flag   If *user-mode* = 0, this data item on exit shows whether the file specified in user-file-spec exists.

	0 = file not found or not searched for
	1 = file was found in a library that was already open
	2 = file was found in a library specified in *user-file-spec*
	3 = file was found as a separate disk file
	If *user-mode* is not 0, then this data item is always 0 on exit.
path-flag	Shows whether *user-file-spec* contained an embedded environment variable that has been expanded in *actual-file-spec* as follows:
	0 = actual-file-spec does not include an expanded environment variable
	1 = *actual-file-spec* contains an expanded environment variable
status-code	Return status:
	0 = success
	1 = the environment variable does not exist
	4 = resulting file-name is illegal
	255 = other error

PC_READ_DRIVE

Returns the current default drive letter.

Syntax:

```
CALL "PC_READ_DRIVE" USING drive
                     RETURNING status-code
```

Parameters:

drive	PIC X.
status-code	See the section *Key*.

Parameters on Entry:

None

Parameters on Exit:

drive   Drive letter, upper- or lower-case.

PC_SET_DRIVE

Sets the default drive letter.

Syntax:

```
CALL "PC_SET_DRIVE" USING drive
                    RETURNING status-code
```

Parameters:

drive   PIC X.
status-code   See the section *Key*.

Parameters on Entry:

drive   Drive letter, upper- or lower-case.

Parameters on Exit:

None

PC_SET_MOUSE_HIDE_AREA

Defines an area ("collision area") where the mouse is to be invisible.

Syntax:

```
CALL "PC_SET_MOUSE_HIDE_AREA" USING mouse-handle
                              collision-area
                    RETURNING status-code
```

Parameters:

mouse-handle	PIC X(4) COMP-X.
collision-area	Group item defined as:
top-row	PIC X(2) COMP-X.
left-col	PIC X(2) COMP-X.
bottom-row	PIC X(2) COMP-X.
right-col	PIC X(2) COMP-X.
status-code	See the section *Key*.

Parameters on Entry:

mouse-handle	Mouse identifier, obtained by earlier call to CBL_INIT_MOUSE.
collision-area	Defines the collision area. Whenever the pointer is in this area, it is hidden. A value of zeros in this item makes the whole screen a collision area. There can be only one collision area at any one time.

Parameters on Exit:

None

PC_SET_MOUSE_SHAPE

Sets the shape of the mouse pointer.

Syntax:

```
CALL "PC_SET_MOUSE_SHAPE" USING mouse-handle
                                reserved-item
                                mouse-ptr-shape
                          RETURNING status-code
```

Parameters:

mouse-handle	PIC X(4) COMP-X.
reserved-item	PIC X(10).

mouse-ptr-shape	Group item defined as:
char_AND_mask	PIC X COMP-X.
attr_AND_mask	PIC X COMP-X.
char_XOR_mask	PIC X COMP-X.
attr_XOR_mask	PIC X COMP-X.
status-code	See the Section *Key*.

Description:

The masks in *mouse-ptr-shape* are bit maps that, applied to a screen position, would superimpose the mouse shape upon it. The pointer shape is formed by PC_SET_MOUSE_SHAPE by ANDing the screen character at the mouse position with *char_AND_mask*, XORing the result with *char_XOR_mask*, and then displaying the result on the screen. The attribute is formed similarly.

See also *Mouse* in *Routines by Category* earlier in this section.

Parameters on Entry:

mouse-handle	Mouse identifier, obtained by earlier call to CBL_INIT_MOUSE.
reserved-item	Reserved for future use
mouse-ptr-shape	The bit maps to create the pointer's desired shape.

Parameters on Exit:

None

PC_TEST_PRINTER

Returns information about the status of a printer.

Syntax:

```
CALL "PC_TEST_PRINTER" USING printer-no
                            printer-status
                      RETURNING status-code
```

Library Routines

Parameters:

printer-no	PIC X COMP-X.
printer-status	PIC X COMP-X.
status-code	See the section *Key*.

Parameters on Entry:

printer-no   Number of the printer to check; must be 0, 1, or 2.

Parameters on Exit:

printer-status   A combination of the following values:
128 (x"80") = not busy
64 (x"40") = acknowledge
32 (x"20") = out of paper
16 (x"10") = selected
8 (x"08")   = I/O error
4 (x"04")   = spare
2 (x"02")   = spare
1 (x"01")   = timeout

Note: These values reflect the status set by the IBM graphics printer. Other printers may return different values.

Call-by-Number Routines

To use a library routine, use the number of the required routine in a COBOL CALL statement.

Routines Available

There are call-by-number routines available to perform the following functions:

84	execute a DOS interrupt
85	examine a one-byte location
86	set a one-byte location
88	output one byte to a hardware port
91	set/read switches and miscellaneous
91/35	run program with given command line
94	examine a two-byte location
95	input one byte from a hardware port
96	input two bytes from a hardware port
97	output two bytes to a hardware port
E5	sound beep
F4	pack data into a byte
F5	unpack data into byte

Note: Some of these routines have options allowing many different functions to be performed.

Descriptions of Routines

Descriptions for all of the call-by-number routines appear in numerical order according to their hex numbers. Each routine is shown in a CALL statement that you could use to call it. The parameters it needs are shown in the USING clause.

Execute a DOS Interrupt

```
CALL x"84" USING interrupt-number, flag, AX-parameter,
    BX-parameter, CX-parameter, DX-parameter
```

where:

interrupt-number   is a PIC X COMP-X field containing the value of the DOS interrupt number.

flag   is a PIC X COMP-X field containing 8 bits set to a 0 or a 1 depending on what is to be placed in the registers AX, BX, CX, and DX.

AX-, BX-, CX-, and DX-parameters   are group items, each consisting of two PIC X COMP-X data items, corresponding to the high and low halves of a 16-bit register. They contain values to be addressed by a register if the corresponding flag bit equals 0 or the value to be placed in the register if the flag bit equals 1.

This routine can be used only for interrupts that accept parameters through the AX, BX, CX, and DX registers. Any interrupt which requires support outside of this constraint, such as control of DS and ES or adjustments to the stack after the interrupt, should be accessed using assembler subprogramming.

The Flag Byte

The least significant 4 bits of the flag byte control the contents of AX, BX, CX, and DX on entry. If the least significant bit is set, AX is loaded with the 16-bit value in the AX parameter. If the least significant bit is not set, then DS:AX addresses the AX parameter. The most significant 4 bits of the flag byte control the contents of AX, BX, CX, and DX on exit. If the most significant bit is set, the value returned in DX by the interrupt is placed in the DX parameter.

On entry to the interrupt call, DS=ES=program address space.

Example

The following example uses the DOS FCB interface to open a file.

```
* dos interrupt number=21h
01 msdos          pic x comp-x value h"21".

* the contents of the parameter funct are to be placed in and
* taken from AX before and after the interrupt.
01 flag           pic x comp-x value h"11".

01 funct.
     02 funct-ah   pic x comp-x.
     02 funct-al   pic x comp-x.
```

```
01 fcb.
     02 filler     pic x value x"00".
     02 filler     pic x(8) value "myfile".
     02 filler     pic x(3) value "dat".
     02 filler     pic x(25).


01 null-param      pic x.


     move 15 to funct-ah
* ah = dos function, open fcb
     call x"84" using msdos, flag, funct,
          null-param, null-param, fcb.


* al = result
     if funct-al is not = 0
          go to file-not-found
     end-if.
```

Read from One- or Two-byte Location

CALL $\left\{ \begin{array}{l} x"85" \\ x"94" \end{array} \right\}$ USING *segment, offset, data-value*

where:

segment   is a PIC 9(5) field containing the segment you want to examine.

offset   is a PIC 9(5) field containing the offset within the segment.

data-value   is a PIC X field for x"85", or PIC XX for x"94", to contain the value returned.

CALL x"85" returns a one-byte value; CALL x"94" returns a two-byte value. The contents found at the location you specify are copied into your program in the field data-value.

Write to One- or Two-byte Location

CALL $\begin{Bmatrix} x"86" \\ x"95" \end{Bmatrix}$ USING *segment*, *offset*, *data-value*

where:

segment   is a PIC 9(5) field containing the segment to which you want to write.

offset   is a PIC 9(5) field containing the offset within the segment.

data-value   is a PIC X field for CALL x"86", or a PIC XX field for CALL x"95", containing the data you want to write.

CALL x"86" writes to a one-byte location; CALL x"95" writes to a two-byte location. The data in data-value is copied to the location you specify.

Read from Hardware Port

CALL $\begin{Bmatrix} x"87" \\ x"96" \end{Bmatrix}$ USING *port*, *data-value*

where:

port   is a PIC 9(5) field containing the port from which to input.

data-value   is a PIC X field for CALL x"87", or PIC XX for CALL x"96", which contains the value returned.

CALL x"87" returns a one-byte value; CALL x"96" returns a two-byte value.

Write to Hardware Port

CALL $\begin{Bmatrix} x"88" \\ x"97" \end{Bmatrix}$ USING *port*, *data-value*

where:

port   is a PIC 9(5) field containing the hardware port to which you want to wrte.

data-value   is a PIC X field for CALL x"88" , or PIC XX for CALL x"97", which contains the value you want to write.

CALL x"88" writes a one-byte value; CALL x"97 writes to a two-byte value. The port is output from your program.

Interprogram Function Calls

CALL   x"91"   USING *result, function-num, parameter*

where:

result   is a PIC X COMP-X field that contains zero if the call is successful, or non-zro if not successful. The numberreturned for non-success ful calls varies accordin to function-num.

function-num   is a PIC COMP-X field that contains one of the values listed below, depending on which function you want.

The format of *parameter* depends on the function.

function-num can contain:

11	to set the COBOL program switches
12	to read the COBOL program switches
13	to et the run-time switches
4	to read the run-time switches
15	to check if a program exists
16	to get the number of linkage parameters
35	to call program under DOS ("4B"call)
46	to enable insertion of null characters
47	to disable insertion of null characters
48	to enable tab insertion
49	to disable tab insertion

Library Routines

Function 11

Sets the COBOL program switches. *parameter*is a group item consisting of two ata items:

- a PIC X COMP-X OCCURS 8 data item that represents switches 0 to 7, inclusive. A 1 in the first element of this item sets switch 0, a 1 in the second element sets switch 1, and so on.

- a PIC X COMP-X data item that contains 1 to set the standard ANSI Debug module on, 0 to switch it off.

To update one switch without affecting the others, you should read the switches with Function 12, update parameter, and then call this function.

Function 12

Reads the COBOL program switches. *parameter* is a group item consisting of two data items:

- a PIC X COMP-X OCCURS 8 data item that represents switches 0 to 7, inclusive, as for Function 11.

- a PIC X COMP-X data item that shows whether the standard ANSI Debug module is enabled as described in Function 11.

Function 13

Sets the run-time switches. *parameter* is a PIC X COMP-X OCCURS 26 field representing run-time switches A to Z, inclusive. The value in the first byte of this item is put into run-time switch A, the second byte into switch B, and so on.

The individual bits in each byte correspond to the digit that can follow a switch-name. For example, to set +S0 and +S5 you set bits 0 and 5 by passing $1 + 32 = 33$ in the "S" byte.

Function 14

Reads the run-time switches. *parameter* is a PIC X COMP-X OCCURS 26 field representing run-time switches A to Z, inclusive, as for Function 13.

Function 15

Checks to see if a program exists. You pass the program name and its length in *parameter*. When the routine exits, *result* is zero if the program is found, non-zero otherwise. *parameter* is a group item consisting of two data items:

- a PIC X COMP-X data item specifying the length in bytes of the data item containing the file-name.

- a PIC X data item of variable length containing the file-name; this data item must be at least 65 bytes long. If the file is found, the routine updates this data item, replacing the file-name that you gave by the full file-name.

If the program file is found, you must then call the program, using the file-name returned.

This call must not be used to check for the existence of data files; use CBL_CHECK_FILE_EXIST instead.

Function 16

Shows how many of the parameters in the CALL statement of the calling program have been transferred to the called subprogram. *parameter* is a PIC X COMP-X field that shows how many parameters have been transferred.

This function can only be used if the program is called from a COBOL program.

Function 35

Performs an EXEC call (like the DOS 4B call) to the program file whose name appears in the parameter field. The command line can be set up using the DISPLAY...UPON COMMAND-LINE syntax (see *Language Reference* chapter for details). The result field is zero if the EXEC call was successful, nonzero otherwise. If the reason for failure is an operating system error and has a number less than 255, that number is returned. Otherwise 255 is returned. *parameter* is a group item consisting of two data items:

■ a PIC X COMP-X field that specifies the number of characters in the file-name. If this field is set to 0, then whatever has been previously written to the command line, using DISPLAY..UPON COMMAND-LINE, is executed.

■ a PIC X field of variable length that contains the file-name of the program file.

Note: If you wish to execute batch (.BAT) or command (.CMD) files with this routine, you must use DISPLAY..UPON COMMAND-LINE.

Example

The following example shows how you can perform a "DIR/W" using function 35:

```
working-storage section.
01 command-lin-string  pic x(80) value "dir/w".
01 result              pic x comp-x.
01 func                pic x comp-x value 35.
01 command-lin.
     03 command-lin-length  pic x comp-x value zero.

procedure division.
main.
     display command-lin-string upon command-line
     call x"91" using result, func, command-lin
     if result = zeros
          display "call worked".
else
          display "call failed".

stop run.
```

Function 46

Enables insertion of a null character x"00" before data characters whose value is less than x"1B" in line sequential files. If you wish to include non-ASCII data in a file then you must enable null insertion. This function allows you to enable null insertion for individual files regardless of the setting of the run-time switch N. *parameter* is the file-identifier specified in the File Description (FD), and must refer to a line sequential file which is currently open. For example:

```
fd payroll-file
    ...
    call x"91" using result, func-num,
                 payroll-file
```

Function 47

Disables insertion of a null character x"00" before data characters whose value is less than x"1B" in line sequential files. This function allows you to disable null insertion for individual files regardless of the setting of the run-time switch N. *parameter* is the file-identifier specified in the File Description (FD) and must refer to a line sequential file which is currently open (see Function 46 above for an example). This function cannot be used if the file is declared as EXTERNAL.

Function 48

Enables insertion of tab characters in line sequential files. On input all tab characters are expanded to the correct number of spaces, while on output to disk, multiple spaces before a tab stop position are contracted to a tab character. This function allows you to enable tab insertion for individual files regardless of the setting of the run-time switch T. *parameter* is the file-identifier specified in the File Description (FD) and must refer to a line sequential file which is currently open. See Function 46 above for an example.

Library Routines

Function 49

Disables insertion of tab characters in line sequential files. On input all tab characters are expanded to the correct number of spaces; on output to disk, spaces are output as spaces. This function allows you to disable tab insertion for individual files regardless of the setting of the run-time switch T. *parameter* is the file-identifier specified in the File Description (FD) and must refer to a line sequential file which is currently open. See Function 46 above for an example.

Control the Screen

CALL   x"A7" USING *function-num, parameter*

where:

function-num   is a PIC X COMP-X field which contains a value indicating the function required:

6 reads the current User attribute
7 sets the current User attribute
16 turns on or off the User attribute

parameter   is a PIC X COMP-X field containing:

(for functions 6 and 7)

the User attribute

(for function 16)

0 to turn the User attribute on
1 to turn the User attribute off

The User attribute is initially off for each program.

The User attribute, if turned on, is used when displaying text upon the screen and supersedes any Screen attribute set for the character positions being used in the display.

When using WRITE to CON:, the output always goes directly to the operating system, using ANSI.SYS.

If the User attribute is not enabled, the Screen attribute currently set for that character position is unaltered.

DISPLAY UPON CRT-UNDER forces highlighting if the User attribute is set on.

DISPLAY SPACE UPON CRT clears the screen to the User attribute for each screen position.

Return Screen Type

```
CALL  x"A7" USING function-num, screen-type
```

where:

function-num   is PIC X COMP-X VALUE 25

screen-type   a PIC X COMP-X field which contains bit
                      settings indicating the type of screen as
                      follows:

                      0 unset = monochrome screen
                      1 reserved
                      2 reserved
                      3 set = EGA-type screen
                      4 set = VGA-type screen
                      5 reserved
                      6 reserved
                      7 reserved

Call x"A7" function 25 returns the current screen type as recognized by the run-time system.

Handle Function Keys

```
CALL  x"B0"  USING function-num, parameter
```

where:

function-num   is a PIC X COMP-X data item and contains a value which determines the function of the subprogram:

0 to set up a function key table
2 to test the status of shift-type keys

parameter   varies for the functions as described below:

(for function 0)   is a table of the form:

PIC X COMP-X

the return byte. Contains the table entry matching the key used or zero if no match is made.

PIC X COMP-X

the length of the next item (in bytes). This must contain the value 0 (which terminates the table), 1 or 2.

PIC X(n)

contains the code sequence produced by the required key. n is the length defined in the length parameter above.

The last two items are repeated once for every key to be detected. The table is terminated by a length parameter of 0.

(for function 2)   is an eight-byte item of the form:

PIC X

> the return byte, which contains bit
> settings indicating the status of the keys
> (1=key pressed, 0=key not pressed) in the
> following order (bit 7 is the high-order bit
> and bit 0 the low-order bit):

Key	Bit
Ins	7
Caps Lock	6
Num Lock	5
Scroll Lock	4
Alt	3
Ctrl	2
Shift (left key) 1	
Shift (right key)	0

PIC X COMP-X

> must be set to 2 before the call is made.

> This item is overwritten by the call, and
> should, therefore, be reset to 2 prior to each
> call.

PIC X(6)

> contents are unimportant

Notes:

■ For the last four of the above keys, this program returns
a 1 only if the key is actually pressed at the time the program
is called; for the other 4 keys, the relevant bit is alternately
set and unset each time the key is pressed.

■ To make these bit settings more accessible to COBOL, you
can use the UNPACK BYTE routine described in this
chapter, or the logical operation routines documented in
Library Routines (Call-by-Name).

■ Effective use of this function requires that the call is repeated at very frequent intervals.

■ CALL x"B0" is specific to an IBM environment. If you intend to use our application in a non-IBM environment, use CALL x"AF".

■ The function key table used by CALL x"AF" is separate from the function key table used by CALL x"B0". Both can be enabled at the same time with all key sequences in the x"B0" table causing the carriage return x"0D" character to be returned to ADIS.

Example - Detecting Function Keys

An ACCEPT statement normally recognizes as control keys only the keys used in data entry (for example, , , ,) and is terminated by the **Enter** key; any other control key is rejected with a beep.

Other control keys and function keys can be made available by calling library routine x"B0" using function 0.

This routine declares a table of key-code sequences, one for each additional key which is to be recognized. Details of the code sequences sent by each key are available in the *IBM Personal Computer Technical Reference Manual*.

After the routine has been called, an ACCEPT statement is terminated by the **Enter** key or by any one of the keys whose code sequence matches an entry in the table. The first byte of the table then contains a number indicaing which entry in the table has been matched; zero indicates that the **Enter** key was used. If the **Enter** key has a entry in the table, then the entry number of tat key is returned rather than zero.

The routine may be called with different tables as often as you require. If the current table is changed (for example, if a key is changed or the length increased), then you don't need to call the routine again.

A table used by a particular program remains enabled for that program until it is superseded by another call to this routine, regardless of how many times this routine is called by other programs in your suite.

Note: You must explicitly set up a table for each program in your suite of programs that uses this facility; passing the table in the Linkage Section is not sufficient.

As long as you know the key-code sent, you can define any key in the table. For example, a table entry with length of 1 and a key-code of PIC X VALUE "C" causes the letter C to end an ACCEPT. You could, therefore, use such a key to "break-out" of an ACCEPT, perform your own processing, and return to the ACCEPT statement. The effect of this is that you have redefined the effect of that particular key.

The result byte is set both on termination of an ACCEPT and on each call to the routine, CBL_READ_KBD_CHAR, when a key in the defined table has been pressed. When this occurs, the character code, x"0D" is returned to the CBL_READ_KBD_CHAR routine, and the result byte indicates which key in the table has been pressed. This means that, you can use CBL_READ_KBD_CHAR to read any single keystroke, including function keys.

For a complete list of code sequences sent by keys, see the technical reference manual for your personal computer.

The following code is an example of how to use the function key call together with CBL_READ_KBD_CHAR:

```
procedure division.
             .     .
             .     .
* Set up function key list
      call x"B0" using B0-function
            B0-parameter-block
      ...
* Read a character from the keyboard
      call "CBL_READ_KBD_CHAR" using char
      if char = x"0D"
* A key defined in the function key table was
* pressed
      evaluate B0-return-byte
```

Library Routines

```
          when 1
          . . .
          when 2
          . . .
       end-evaluate
       . . .
     else
       if char = x"00"
       * A function key not defined in the table was
* pressed
             call "CBL_READ_KBD_CHAR" using char
* char contains the key's scan code
          . . .
       else
* char contains a character
       end-if
     end-if.
```

Sound the Beep

CALL x"E5"

This routine causes a beep of about 1/8 second duration.

Pack Byte

CALL x"F4" USING *byte*, *array*

where:

byte   is a PIC X COMP-X field that contains the new byte.

array   is a PIC X COMP-X OCCURS 8 field that contains the
              eight bytes to be packed.

The routine takes the eight fields from *array* and uses the least
significant bit of each byte to form *byte*. The first occurrence in
array becomes the most significant bit of *byte* (bit 7).

Unpack Byte

```
CALL  x"F5"  USING byte, array
```

where:

byte is a PIC X COMP-X field that contains the byte to be unpacked.

array is a PIC X COMP-X OCCURS 8 field that contains the unpacked bits.

The routine takes the eight bits of byte and moves them to the corresponding occurrence within array

Chapter 3

ADIS

Overview

ADIS is a run-time support module which provides for Screen Section and enhanced ACCEPT/DISPLAY syntax. Calls can be made from the COBOL application to ADIS to configure it at run time; for example, to enable function keys.

Enhanced ACCEPT/DISPLAY

The enhanced ACCEPT/DISPLAY syntax provides functionality beyond the standard ANSI ACCEPT syntax, which enables you to input a data-item or accept the day, date or time into a data-item, and the ANSI DISPLAY syntax, which allows you to output literals and the contents of data items.

With the enhanced ACCEPT/DISPLAY syntax supported by ADIS, you can specify screen position and screen attributes. It also makes it possible to do either single-field or multiple-field AC-CEPT operations. For multiple-field ACCEPT operations, FILLER describes the number of character positions to skip over to the next field. In a DISPLAY operation, FILLER defines the number of spaces between literals. All areas defined as FILLER are unaffected by the ACCEPT or DISPLAY operation.

Screen Section

The Screen Section is a section in the Data Division containing one or more screen definitions. A screen definition may contain fields, groups, text and attributes. Fields may have edited picture strings and may also have such features as NO-ECHO, JUSTIFIED RIGHT, BLANK WHEN ZERO, etc. How the screen definitions are ACCEPTed and DISPLAYed in the Procedure Division is handled by ADIS.

Configuration

ADIS can be configured to affect the behavior of ACCEPT and DISPLAY statements at run time. You can configure ADIS by making calls to ADIS from the COBOL application at run-time.

Operation

This section describes how Enhanced ACCEPT and DISPLAY statements are handled at run time when used with:

- Elementary data items

- Group items

- Screen Section items

The term field used in relation to screen handling refers to an area on the screen that corresponds to a single data-item during accept and display operations.

Single Field ACCEPT and DISPLAY Statements

This section describes how ACCEPT and DISPLAY statements in the following format are handled at run-time:

```
display data-item at xxyy ...
accept data-item at xxyy ...
```

where data-item is an elementary item defined in the Data Division of your program and xxyy specifies the position on the screen (xx=line, yy=column) where the DISPLAY or ACCEPT field starts. The length of the field is governed by the length and type of data-item, and the SIZE clause.

DISPLAY Statements

The following sections describe the way that the DISPLAY statement functions.

Format of Displayed Data

When a data item is displayed on the screen, it occupies the same number of characters on the screen as it does bytes in memory.

Examples

Data Item Description	Size on Screen	Comment
X(5)	5 characters	
N(5)	10 characters	Each PIC N character occupies 2 bytes in memory
9(5)	5 characters	
99.99	5 characters	
Z(4)9	5 characters	
99V99	4 characters	V is an implied decimal point and so is not displayed on the screen

S9(4)	4 characters	The sign is implied and so is not displayed on the screen
S9(4) SIGN LEADING SEPARATE	5 characters	
9(4) COMP	2 characters	COMP fields are stored in binary; a 9(4) COMP field occupies 2 bytes in memory

As can be seen from the above examples, it is only really sensible to display fields defined as USAGE DISPLAY which do not contain implied signs or decimal points. When the field is displayed, it is copied byte-for-byte from the data item onto the screen at the required position.

Note: ANSI DISPLAY operations do convert non-USAGE DISPLAY numeric items to USAGE DISPLAY before displaying.

Control Sequences in Displayed Data

Control sequences cannot be embedded in the data that is displayed. If you do embed control codes (that is, ASCII codes less than 32) into the data, the IBM graphics character corresponding to that code is displayed. For example, displaying ASCII code 7 results in a diamond character being displayed instead of sounding the bell. (For some products developed for other environments, such characters are replaced by a space.) All highlighting, cursor control, etc., must be done through the syntax provided.

Displaying Highlighted Text

If you use the CRT-UNDER phrase in a DISPLAY statement, the data item is displayed highlighted. Depending on your CRT, use of the CRT-UNDER phrase may cause data items to be displayed underlined or in reverse-video.

ACCEPT Statements

The following sections describe how the ACCEPT statement is executed on different types of fields.

Alphanumeric Fields

The term Alphanumeric Field is used here to cover all alphanumeric, alphabetic and alphanumeric-edited fields. For the purposes of an ACCEPT, an alphanumeric-edited field is treated as an alphanumeric field of the same length. Any insertion symbols such as "/" or "0" are ignored and treated as an X. Therefore, a field defined as PIC XX0XX0XX is treated as if it was specified as PIC X(8).

If the field is defined as alphabetic, only the characters "A" to "Z", "a" to "z" and space are allowed into the field.

The cursor is initially placed at the start of the field.

As data is entered into the field, the cursor is advanced to the next character. The cursor can be moved back over the data in the field using the cursor keys, and editing functions such as backspace, delete, etc. are provided. By default, the **Ins** key is set up to toggle between insert mode and replace mode.

Fixed Format Data Entry

This is also known as formatted mode. It can best be described as "What you see is what you get". As each key is pressed, the field is automatically reformatted to conform to the picture string. Therefore, ADIS tries to ensure that the field always looks on the screen as it is stored in the Data Division, and its size is the same as the size of the data item.

Therefore, as with the DISPLAY statement, it is only really sensible to accept fields that are defined as USAGE DISPLAY with no implied sign or decimal point.

During data entry, characters other than numeric digits, +, - and the decimal point character are rejected. Insertion characters in edited fields are automatically skipped over as the cursor is moved backwards and forwards. Any sign indicator is automatically modified if a "+" or "-" is pressed, regardless of where the cursor is in the field.

Zeros are allowed as insertion characters only as a leading symbol before a decimal point, or as a trailing symbol following a decimal point. For example, PIC 0.9999 and PIC 999.90 are valid, but PIC 0.0009 and PIC 999,000 are not.

Data entry of simple numerics and numeric-edited fields with no zero suppression is similar to that for alphanumeric fields, except that insert mode is not supported in numeric and numeric-edited fields. If the decimal point character is pressed in a simple numeric field, the digits are right justified. For example, a field defined as PIC 9(5) which initially contains zeros is accepted as follows (underlined characters indicate cursor position):

Initial display	00000
Pressing 1 will give	10000
Pressing 2 will give	12000
Pressing 4 will give	12400
Pressing backspace will give	12000
Pressing "." will give	00012

Data entry into zero-suppressed fields is handled differently. The cursor is initially placed on the first character position that is not zero-suppressed. If all the digits before the decimal point are suppressed, the cursor is positioned on the decimal point itself.

While the cursor is to the left of the decimal point (that is, in the integer part of the field), the cursor moves to the right as digits are entered until the decimal point is reached. Any further digits are inserted immediately before the decimal point until all the integer places are filled. The cursor is then automatically moved to the first decimal digit and advances as the decimal digits are entered.

If you wish to enter digits after the decimal point when there are integer places still unfilled, the decimal point (.) must be entered.

For example, assume that a numeric-edited data field is defined as PIC ZZZ99.99 and initially contains zeros, the field will be displayed as follows during the ACCEPT:

Initial display	0̲0.00
Pressing 1 gives	10̲.00
Pressing 2 gives	12̲.00
Pressing 3 gives	123̲.00
Pressing 4 gives	1234̲.00
Pressing backspace gives	123̲.00
Pressing 5 gives	1235̲.00
Pressing 6 gives	12356̲.00
Pressing 7 gives	12356.70̲
Pressing 8 gives	12356.78̲

If you want to enter 123.45 into the same field, the field appears as follows:

Initial display	0̲0.00
Pressing 1 gives	10̲.00
Pressing 2 gives	12̲.00
Pressing 3 gives	123̲.00
Pressing "." gives	123.0̲0
Pressing 4 gives	123.40̲
Pressing 5 gives	123.45̲

Fixed format mode is only allowed on numeric-edited data items of length up to 32 characters. If they are longer than 32 characters, they are automatically handled in free-format mode as described below. Fields are also automatically treated as free-format if a SIZE clause is specified in the ACCEPT statement.

Free-format Data Entry

During data entry into a free-format field, the field is treated as an alphanumeric field of the appropriate length. It is only when the user leaves the field that it is reformatted to comply with the picture string. Any characters other than the digits, the sign character and the decimal point character are discarded.

Fields occupy the same number of characters on the screen as they do bytes in memory, with the exception that an additional character is allocated for implied signs and decimal points. Therefore, a data item defined as PIC S99V99 occupies six characters on the screen in free-format mode as opposed to four characters in fixed-format mode.

Data entry is the same as for alphanumeric fields.

If an enhanced ACCEPT statement is being used, the clauses SPACE-FILL, ZERO-FILL, LEFT-JUSTIFY, RIGHT-JUSTIFY and TRAILING-SIGN are applicable only to free-format non-edited fields (and are ignored with fixed-format fields). See the description of the ACCEPT statement in the *Language Reference* chapter for further details of these clauses.

General Notes

These notes concern the accepting of data into fields:

■ If a field is too long to fit on one line on the screen, it is split into separate sub-fields at run-time. Each sub-field fits entirely onto one line. The cursor automatically auto-skips into the next sub-field at the end of one sub-field, regardless of the setting of any auto-skip controls.

For example, if you accept a data item that is PIC X(190) at line 1, column 1 and the screen is only 80 characters wide, the field is broken into three sub-fields, two with 80 characters and one with 30 characters.

■ If a field extends beyond the end of the screen, the action taken depends on the type of field:

■ Alphanumeric fields are truncated to a size that fits on the screen.

■ Numeric and numeric-edited fields are treated as if they were defined as FILLER (that is, not a field) and are ignored.

■ As most terminals scroll upwards as a result of a character appearing in the final character position of the screen (bottom right) it is not possible to use this character position as part of an ACCEPT.

Microsoft COBOL V2.2 Emulation

The style of data entry into numeric and numeric-edited fields in Microsoft's COBOL Version 2.2 is quite different from the style used in this product. The main difference is that decimal points and implied signs are treated as if they were specified as "." and "-". Therefore, a PIC S99V99 field is treated as if it was specified as a -99.99 field during execution of an ACCEPT or DISPLAY statement under Microsoft COBOL V2.2. All ACCEPT and DISPLAY statements behave as if the phrase MODE IS BLOCK has been specified.

The other major difference between the behavior of this COBOL system and Microsoft COBOL V2.2 during execution of a numeric ACCEPT is that Microsoft COBOL V2.2 accepts data from right-to-left and this COBOL accepts data from left-to-right.

Displaying or Accepting Group Items

When displaying or accepting group items, each elementary item within the group is treated as a separate field. If an elementary item is defined as FILLER, it is simply used as a positioning item of the appropriate size (that is, you cannot accept into FILLER items or display FILLER items).

Displaying Group Items

Consider the following group item:

```
01 display-item.
      03 display-item-1          pic x(20).
      03 filler                  pic x(35).
      03 display-item-2          pic 9(10).
      03 filler                  pic x(105).
      03 display-item-3          pic z(4)9.
```

If the following statement is executed on a screen 80 characters wide:

```
display display-item at 0101
```

`display-item-1` is displayed at row 1, column 1,
`display-item-2` is displayed at row 1, column 56, and
`display-item-3` is displayed at row 3, column 11

All other areas of the screen are unaffected by the DISPLAY. FILLER items do not cause any data to be displayed on the screen. Consequently, data already on the screen in the positions defined by each FILLER is not altered in any way by the DISPLAY.

If a data item is defined as follows :

```
01 data-item.
   03 data-char        pic x occurs 2000.
```

and the following statement is executed:

```
display data-item at 0101
```

then this is treated as a display of 2000 fields, each defined as PIC X, which is unlikely to be what you require. To avoid this, either redefine `data-item` as a PIC X(2000) and display that or use the MODE IS BLOCK clause described below.

Accepting into Group Items

When accepting into a group item, each field is accepted into as described for single-field ACCEPT statements earlier in this section.

Unless you explicitly position the cursor (see *The CURSOR IS Clause* later in this section), the cursor is initially placed at the start of the first field.

When the end of a field is reached, the cursor is normally advanced to the beginning of the next field automatically. The keys set up for next and previous field operations (usually tab and back-tab) move you between the individual fields. In addition, the cursor keys move you around the fields.

The MODE IS BLOCK Clause

If the MODE IS BLOCK clause is added to an ACCEPT or DIS-PLAY of a group item, the group item is treated as if it was an elementary item of the total size of the group item.

For example, if the following statement is executed:

```
display display-item at 0101 mode is block.
```

where `display-item` is as defined in the section *Displaying Group Items*, `display-item` is treated as if it was an elementary item defined as:

```
01 display-item          pic x(175).
```

Consequently, the contents of the FILLER items are also displayed.

The CURSOR IS Clause

This feature allows you to specify precisely where in a field you want the cursor to be positioned at the start of the ACCEPT operation, and returns where the cursor was left at the end of an ACCEPT operation. If you do not specify a CURSOR IS clause in your program, the cursor is always initially positioned at the start of the first field for every ACCEPT operation.

The CURSOR IS clause is defined in the SPECIAL-NAMES paragraph, as follows :

```
special-names.
    cursor is cursor-position.
```

where cursor-position is a field defined in your Working-Storage section as follows :

```
01 cursor-position.
    03 cursor-row            pic 99.
    03 cursor-column         pic 99.
```

where:

cursor-row   Specifies the row the cursor is positioned on. Valid values are between 1 and the number of lines on the screen.

cursor-column   Specifies the column the cursor is positioned on. Valid values are between 1 and the number of columns on the screen.

Whenever an ACCEPT statement is executed, ADIS attempts to initially position the cursor at the position specified in cursor-position. If the position specified is invalid (that is, either cursor-row or cursor-column does not contain a valid value), the cursor is positioned at the start of the first field on the screen.

If the value in cursor-position is valid, ADIS searches through all of the fields to see if the requested cursor position lies within one of them. If it does, the cursor is positioned at the required point. If it does not, then the cursor is positioned at the start of the first field. Therefore, if you want the cursor to be positioned at the start of the first field, set both cursor-row and cursor-column to 1.

Where the defined position is on a suppressed character or insertion symbol in a numeric edited field, the cursor moves to the first available character to the right. If there is no further data item, the cursor returns to the first data item on the screen.

When the ACCEPT is terminated, if the value in cursor-position at the start of the ACCEPT was valid, the position of the cursor when the terminating key is pressed is returned in cursor-position. Note, however, that this may not be the same position as the current cursor position, since ADIS usually moves the cursor to the end of the field upon termination of an ACCEPT operation to allow relative positioned ACCEPT statements to start at the correct point on the screen.

If the value in cursor-position at the start of the ACCEPT was invalid, then, when the ACCEPT is terminated, the contents of cursor-position are unchanged.

One example of the use of this facility is that in menu-type operations, the operator need only move the cursor to a position on the screen corresponding to the selection required. The operator's choice can be determined by the returned value of cursor-position.

Large Screens

Screens larger than 25 lines can be detected by your COBOL system. On a screen larger than 25 lines the +C switch should be used at run time.

Programs using ANSI ACCEPT/DISPLAY statements, enhanced ACCEPT/DISPLAY syntax, Screen Section and the COBOL system library routines should run correctly on large screens. It is worth noting, however, that if an application is developed for a screen larger than the screen it is run on, then it results in the loss of the extra lines, or, in single field ACCEPT/DISPLAY statements, it results in the screen being scrolled up by one line.

ADIS Run Time Configuration

One of the powerful features of ADIS is that it can be configured to tailor the behavior of ACCEPT and DISPLAY statements. This section describes features of ADIS that are not available via CO-BOL syntax, but can be accessed with the x"AF" COBOL system library routine.

All of these features are accessed by the following call statement:

```
call x"af" using set-bit-pairs parameter-block
```

where the parameters are defined as follows:

```
01 set-bit-pairs              pic 9(2) comp-x value 1.
01 parameter-block.
      03 bit-pair-setting     pic 9(2) comp-x.
      03 filler               pic x value "2".
      03 bit-pair-number      pic 9(2) comp-x.
      03 filler               pic 9(2) comp-x value 1.
```

The values to be set for the fields bit-pair-setting and bit-pair-number are given in each of the descriptions below.

With all x"AF" calls, if an error occurs, the first parameter is set to the value 255.

The functions available using this facility are as follows:

■ Enable/disable pre-display

■ Enable/disable display of the ADIS indicators

■ Enable/disable display of ADIS error messages

■ Enable/disable auto-skip between fields

■ Enable/disable input data case conversion

■ Enable/disable password concealment

Enable/Disable Pre-display

This allows you to control whether or not the initial contents of fields are pre-displayed before any data entry is allowed when an ACCEPT statement is executed.

Note: The pre-display of fields defined as fixed format numeric or numeric-edited cannot be turned off.

The fields in *parameter-block* should be set as follows:

bit-pair-number must be set to 76.

bit-pair-setting should be set to one of the following values:

0   Only fixed-format numeric and fixed-format numeric-edited fields are pre-displayed.

1   Only numeric fields and fixed-format numeric-edited fields are pre-displayed.

2   A field is pre-displayed as soon as the cursor is moved into it.

3   All of the fields in the ACCEPT are

pre-displayed before any data entry is
allowed. The default.

Example

The following code will turn off pre-display of fields for all following ACCEPT operations:

```
move 76 TO bit-pair-number
move 0 TO bit-pair-setting
call x"af" using set-bit-pairs parameter-block
```

Enable/Disable Display of the ADIS Indicators

These routines allow you to enable or disable the display of the
indicators that ADIS displays during an ACCEPT to indicate
insert/replace mode, autoclear mode or "off end of field". By
default, these indicators are displayed.

There are different calls to control each of these indicators, but
they all have the same format.

The fields in *parameter-block* should be set as follows:

bit-pair-number should be set to one of the following:

> 56 To control the Insert/Replace mode indicator
> 57 To control the "Off end of field" indicator
> 58 To control the "Autoclear" indicator

bit-pair-setting should be set to one of the following:

> 0   The indicator is displayed if necessary.
> The default.
>
> 3   The indicator is never displayed.

Example

The following code will disable display of the insert/replace
indicator and enable display of the "Off end of field" indicator.

```
move 56 to bit-pair-number
move 3 to bit-pair-setting
call x"AF" using set-bit-pairs parameter-block
move 57 to bit-pair-number
move 0 to bit-pair-setting
call x"AF" using set-bit-pairs parameter-block
```

Enable/Disable Display of ADIS Error Messages

This routine allows you to enable or disable the display of the messages that ADIS may output during execution of an ACCEPT statement. By default, these messages are displayed.

The fields in *parameter-block* should be set as follows:

bit-pair-number must be set to 44.

bit-pair-setting should be set to one of the following values:

0   Error messages are never displayed, but the bell is rung. Invalid data entered into a numeric or numeric- edited field in free-format mode is not reported as an error.

1   Error messages are never displayed, but the bell is rung. Invalid data entered into a numeric or numeric-edited field in free format mode is reported as an error by ringing the bell.

2   Error messages are displayed and the bell is rung if the appropriate error occurs. Invalid data entered into a numeric or numeric-edited field in free-format mode is not reported as an error.

3   Error messages are displayed and the bell is rung if the appropriate error occurs. Invalid data entered into a numeric or numeric-edited field in free-format mode is reported as an error by ringing the bell.

Example

The following code will disable the display of error messages and disable the reporting of invalid data in numeric and numeric-edited fields.

```
move 44 TO bit-pair-number
move 0 TO bit-pair-setting
call x"af" using set-bit-pairs parameter-block
```

Enable/Disable Auto-skip Between Fields

This routine allows you to control circumstances in which auto-skip to a following or preceding field may occur, during execution of an ACCEPT statement.

The fields in *parameter-block* should be set as follows:

> *bit-pair-number* must be set to 81.

> *bit-pair-setting* should be set to one of the following values:

1	No auto-skip. An explicit field-tab or cursor key (but not Backspace) must be used to move between fields.
3	Auto-skip enabled. Any cursor movement or a character key will cause auto-skip to the next field if at end of the current field. The default.

Example

The following code will disable auto-skip between fields:

```
move 81 TO bit-pair-number
move 1 TO bit-pair-setting
call x"af" using set-bit-pairs parameter-block
```

Enable/Disable Input Data Case Conversion

This routine allows you to control whether lower-case ASCII characters are automatically converted to upper-case on entry during execution of an ACCEPT statement.

The fields in *parameter-block* should be set as follows:

bit-pair-number must be set to 85.

bit-pair-setting should be set to one of the following values:

0	No case conversion occurs. (The default.)
1	Lower case alphabetic input data is converted to upper case on entry.

Example

The following code will enable conversion to upper case of all alphabetic input.

```
move 85 to bit-pair-number
move 1 to bit-pair-setting
call x"af" using set-bit-pairs parameter-block
```

Enable/Disable Password Concealment

This routine allows you to control whether characters input when an ACCEPT statement is executed should be echoed to the screen, or not.

The fields in *parameter-block* should be set as follows:

bit-pair-number must be set to 84.

bit-pair-setting should be set to one of the following values:

0	Input is echoed to the screen. (The default.)

| 1 | Input is not echoed to the screen for the next ACCEPT statement encountered only. |

| 2 | Input is not echoed to the screen for any following ACCEPT statements until it is re-enabled. |

Example

The following code will conceal the input for the next ACCEPT statement only:

```
move 84 to bit-pair-number
move 1 to bit-pair-setting
call x"af" using set-bit-pairs parameter-block
```

Select Timeout Units

This routine allows you to determine whether the timeout value is interpreted as seconds or tenths of a second.

The fields in *parameter-block* should be set as follows:

bit-pair-number must be set to 14.

bit-pair-setting should be set to one of the following values:

| 0 | Units are seconds. |

| 1 | Units are tenths of a second. |

Timeout Reset Control

This routine allows you to control whether the timer is reset every time a character is entered, or times out after the specified period anyway.

The fields in *parameter-block* should be set as follows:

bit-pair-number must be set to 15.

bit-pair-setting should be set to one of the following values:

0   Timer is never reset. Timeout occurs after the specified time from the start of the accept.

1   The timer is reset each time a character is entered.

Screen Section

The Screen Section provides screen handling facilities for use with ACCEPT and DISPLAY statements. It allows the display of non-scrolling areas of the screen as defined in the screen section. A screen section entry is a *screen description*. It is similar in appearance to a data description but defines a *screen item* or area of the screen rather than an area in memory. Many screen items describe only the layout of fields within a field on the screen, and are never referenced explicitly.

The screen section entry construct, and use of screen-names with ACCEPT and DISPLAY statements, are documented in the *Language Reference* chapter of this book.

Screen Descriptions define areas on the screen. Each entry consists of a level number, an optional screen name, and various optional clauses relating to the positioning of fields as well as to console functions.

The options which can be used in a screen section entry or in a suitable ACCEPT or DISPLAY statement are described below. The following table shows where each option is permitted:

Screen Clauses/ Screen Options/ Data Description Clauses	SCREEN SECTION FIELDS				WITH PHRASE		
	Input	Output	Update	Literal	Accept	Display	Control
AUTO	X		X		X		X
BACKGROUND-COLOR	X	X	X	X	X	X	X
BELL	X	X	X	X	X	X	X
BLANK	X	X	X	X		X	X
BLANK WHEN ZERO	X	X	X				
BLINK	X	X	X	X	X	X	X
COLUMN	X	X	X	X			
ERASE	X	X	X	X	X		
FOREGROUND-COLOR	X	X	X	X	X	X	X
FULL	X		X		X		X
GRID	X	X	X	X	X	X	X
HIGHLIGHT	X	X	X	X	X	X	X
JUSTIFIED	X	X	X				X
LEFT-JUSTIFY					X		
LEFTLINE	X	X	X	X	X	X	X
LINE	X	X	X	X			
LOWLIGHT	X	X	X	X	X	X	
OCCURS	X	X	X				
OVERLINE	X	X	X	X	X	X	X
PROMPT	X		X		X		X
REQUIRED	X		X		X		X
REVERSE-VIDEO	X	X	X	X	X	X	X
RIGHT-JUSTIFY					X		
SECURE	X		X		X		X
SIGN	X	X	X				
SIZE	X	X	X	X	X	X	
SPACE-FILL					X		
TRAILING -SIGN					X		X
UNDERLINE	X	X	X	X	X	X	

Screen Section Option Descriptions

In the descriptions which follow, the Format definitions use these conventions:

<u>UNDERLINED</u> words in upper case are required
UPPER CASE words which are not underlined may be written or not as the programmer wishes.
Lower-case words represent names which the programmer will devise.
Words separated by | are alternatives.
Words enclosed between <> are options which may be included but which will change the meaning of the phrase.

The AUTO Clause

The AUTO clause automatically terminates an ACCEPT operation of the screen item when the last character position is keyed. No explicit terminator key is necessary. If AUTO is used at a group level it applies to all subordinate items.

Format: <u>AUTO</u>

The BACKGROUND-COLOR Clause

The BACKGROUND-COLOR clause specifies the background color of the screen item. If the clause is used at a group level it applies to all subordinate items. The color is specified as an integer. The colors and corresponding values are:

0	black
1	blue
2	green
3	cyan
4	red
5	magenta
6	brown or yellow
7	white

The default color is black.

Format: <u>BACKGROUND-COLOR</u> IS integer

The BELL Clause

The BELL clause causes an audible alarm to occur each time the item containing the clause is displayed. BELL may only be used with elementary items.

Format: <u>BELL</u>

The BLANK LINE or SCREEN Clause

During a DISPLAY operation, each subsidiary item within a screen-name is displayed according to source sequence. At an item with BLANK LINE, the screen is cleared to spaces from the beginning of the line to the end of the line. The cursor position is not changed. BLANK LINE may only be used for elementary items. At an item with BLANK SCREEN, the entire screen is cleared to spaces and the cursor repositioned to line 1, column 1.

Format: <u>BLANK</u> <u>LINE</u> | <u>SCREEN</u>

The BLANK WHEN ZERO Clause

The BLANK WHEN ZERO clause causes the blanking of a screen item when its value is zero. This clause is allowed only with fields that are numeric or numeric-edited.

Format: <u>BLANK</u> WHEN <u>ZERO</u>

The BLINK Clause

The BLINK clause causes the screen item to blink when it appears on the screen. If the clause is used at a group level it applies to all suitable subordinate items.

Format: <u>BLINK</u>

The COLUMN Clause

The COLUMN clause specifies the column at which the screen item starts on the screen. COL is an abbreviation for COLUMN. If "+" or "-" is specified then the column number is relative to that at which the preceding screen item ends, otherwise the clause gives an absolute column number, which defaults to 1 if no number is given. If a position is specified which is off the screen, wraparound occurs.

Format: COLUMN <NUMBER IS <+ | -> identifier | integer>

The CONTROL Clause

The CONTROL clause allows attributes associated with a screen section item to be defined at run time. Options which may be used with CONTROL are shown on page 3-21.
If the clause is used at a group level it applies to all suitable subordinate items.

Format: CONTROL is identifier

The ERASE Clause

The ERASE clause clears part of the line or the screen starting at the cursor position. When ERASE EOL is specified, blanking occurs from the start of the screen data element to the end of the line. When ERASE EOS is specified, blanking occurs from the start of the screen data element to the end of the screen. If neither EOS or EOL are specified, only the screen data element is cleared. The ERASE clause can be specified only for elementary items. The clause is ignored in an ACCEPT.

Format: ERASE EOL | EOS

The FOREGROUND-COLOR Clause

The FOREGROUND-COLOR clause specifies the foreground color of the screen item. If the clause is used at a group level it applies to all suitable subordinate items. The color is specified as an integer. The colors and corresponding values are:

0	black
1	blue
2	green
3	cyan
4	red
5	magenta
6	brown or yellow
7	white

The default color is white.

Format: <u>FOREGROUND-COLOR</u> IS integer I identifier

The FULL Clause

The FULL clause specifies that the operator must either leave the item completely empty or fill it entirely with data. If the clause is used at a group level it applies to all suitable subordinate items. The FULL clause is not effective if a function key is used to terminate the ACCEPT.

Format: <u>FULL</u>

The GRID Clause

The GRID clause causes each character of the screen item to have a vertical line on its left-hand side when the item appears on the screen. Each line is within the character position. If the clause is used at a group level it applies to all suitable subordinate items. If this clause is used on a system which does not support characters with vertical left-hand lines it has no effect.

Format: <u>GRID</u>

The HIGHLIGHT Clause

The HIGHLIGHT Clause causes the screen item to appear in high intensity mode when it appears on the screen. If the clause is used at a group level it applies to all suitable subordinate items.

Format: HIGHLIGHT

The JUSTIFIED Clause

The JUSTIFIED Clause specifies non-standard positioning of data within a screen item when data is either moved to it or entered into it.

Format: JUSTIFIED RIGHT

The LEFTLINE Clause

The LEFTLINE Clause causes the leftmost character of the screen item to have a vertical line on its left-hand side when the item appears on the screen. Each line is within the character position. If the clause is used at a group level it applies to all suitable subordinate items. On a system which does not support characters with vertical left-hand lines this clause has no effect.

Format: LEFTLINE

The LINE Clause

The LINE Clause specifies the line at which the screen item starts on the screen. If "+" or "-" is specified then the line number is relative to that at which the preceding screen item ends, otherwise the clause gives an absolute line number, which defaults to 1 if no number is given. If a position is specified which is off the screen, the ACCEPT or DISPLAY is truncated.

Format: LINE <NUMBER IS <+ | -> identifier | integer>

The LOWLIGHT Clause

The LOWLIGHT Clause specifies that the field is to appear on the screen with the lowest intensity. LOWLIGHT may be specified only for an elementary screen description entry.

Format: <u>LOWLIGHT</u>

The OCCURS Clause

The OCCURS Clause eliminates the need for separate entries for repeated screen items and supplies information required for the application of subscripts or indices. If OCCURS applies to the screen item, then a receiving item must have the same number of OCCURS; a sending item must have either no OCCURS at all, or the same number of OCCURS, and the DEPENDING phrase must not be used.

Format: <u>OCCURS</u> integer TIMES

The OVERLINE Clause

The OVERLINE Clause causes every character of the screen item to have a horizontal line above it when the item appears on the screen. The line is within the character position. If the clause is used at a group level it applies to all suitable subordinate items. This clause has no effect on a system which does not support overlining.

Format: <u>OVERLINE</u>

The PICTURE Clause

The PICTURE Clause describes the length, general characteristics and editing requirements of a screen item. The FROM, TO and USING phrases identify the source of data for display and the destination of data accepted; USING is equivalent to the TO and FROM phrases both specifying the same identifier. The PICTURE clause is allowed only with elementary items.

Format: <u>PICTURE</u> IS character-string
            <<u>FROM</u> identifier | literal>
            <<u>TO</u> identifier>
            <<u>USING</u> identifier>

The PROMPT Clause

The PROMPT Clause causes the empty character positions in the screen item to be marked on the screen during an ACCEPT operation while the system is ready to accept operator-keyed data into that item. If the clause is used at a group level it applies to all suitable subordinate items.

Format: <u>PROMPT</u> <<u>CHARACTER</u> IS identifier | literal>

The identifier or literal must be a single character.

The PROTECT Clause

The PROTECT Clause specifies that input to an ACCEPT item is to be prevented. It can only be used for an elementary screen description entry.

Format: <u>PROTECT</u>

The REQUIRED Clause

The REQUIRED Clause specifies that the operator must not leave the screen item empty. If the clause is used at a group level it applies to all suitable subordinate items.

Format: <u>REQUIRED</u>

The REVERSE-VIDEO Clause

The REVERSE-VIDEO Clause causes the screen item to be displayed in reverse-video. If the clause is used at a group level it applies to all suitable subordinate items.

Format: <u>REVERSE-VIDEO</u>

The SECURE Clause

The SECURE Clause prevents operator-keyed data from appearing on the screen. SECURE and NO-ECHO are equivalent. For input fields, only spaces and the cursor appear in the screen item; for update fields, the original contents of the field will be displayed but will not be altered. If the clause is used at a group level it applies to all suitable subordinate items.

Format: <u>SECURE</u> | <u>NO-ECHO</u>

The SIGN Clause

The SIGN Clause specifies the position and representation of the operational sign. This clause is allowed only with input, output and update fields whose pictures contain the character 'S'. It is recommended that the SEPARATE option be used when the SIGN clause is used in a screen description; if SEPARATE is not used, a SIGN denoted by 'S' in a PICTURE clause appears as an overpunch (which changes the character shown). SIGN is allowed only with elementary items.

Format: <u>SIGN</u> IS <u>LEADING</u> | <u>TRAILING</u> <<u>SEPARATE</u>>

The SIZE Clause

The SIZE Clause specifies the current size of the screen item. It may only be used with elementary screen items. The identifier must be an unsigned numeric integer and must not be subject to an OCCURS clause.

Format: <u>SIZE</u> IS identifier | integer

The UNDERLINE Clause

The UNDERLINE Clause causes the screen item to be underlined when it appears on the screen. This clause has no effect if the system does not support underline. If the clause is used at a group level it applies to all suitable subordinate items.

Format: UNDERLINE

The VALUE Clause

The VALUE Clause specifies literal information for display on the screen. This clause is allowed only with elementary items that have no PICTURE clause. The literal must be non numeric.

Format: VALUE IS literal

The ZERO-FILL Clause

The ZERO-FILL Clause causes trailing prompt characters to be replaced by zeros instead of spaces. The clause is allowed only with input and update fields that are alphabetic or alphanumeric.

Format: ZERO-FILL

Screen Section ACCEPT and DISPLAY Statements

ACCEPT and DISPLAY operations involving Screen Section items are treated like any other ACCEPT or DISPLAY operation, but with one important difference. Consider the following code:

```
working-storage section.
01 item-a            pic 9(5).
01 item-b            pic 9(10).
01 item-c            pic x(10).

screen section.
01 demo-screen.
     03 blank screen.
     03 line 1 column 1 pic z(4)9 from item-a.
     03 line 3 column 1 pic 9(10) to item-b.
     03 line 5 column 1 pic x(10) using item-c.
```

When this code is compiled, the compiler sets up a work area for each Screen Section 01 level item (record). Therefore, in this example, a work area is set up for demo-screen large enough to hold the data for the three fields.

When the statement

```
display demo-screen
```

is executed, the contents of item-a and item-c are moved from Working-Storage into the work area, and then the data in the work area for these two fields is displayed on the screen.

When the statement

```
accept demo-screen
```

is executed, data is accepted into the work area for Item-B and Item-C and then the data for these two fields is moved from the work area into the Working-Storage.

It is important to note that moves from the Data Division to the work area occur only on execution of a DISPLAY statement, and moves from the work area to the Data Division occur only during execution of an ACCEPT statement. Therefore, if two ACCEPT statements are executed one after another with no intervening DISPLAY statement, the initial contents of the fields at the start of the second accept are that which was put into the work area during the previous accept not the current contents of the Data Division items.

Another implication of this is that a field should not be defined as numeric-edited in both the Data Division section and the Screen Section. This results in numeric-edited to numeric-edited moves being generated by the compiler to move the Data Division item into the work area and back again. The action of such moves is undefined and has unpredictable results. This is the case even if both the Data Division item and the Screen Section item have the same picture.

Hence, if the following lines are coded in your program:

```
working-storage section.
01 ws-item                 pic zz9.99 value 1.23

screen section.
01 demo-screen.
     03 pic zz9.99 using ws-item.

procedure division.
     display demo-screen.
```

the result of the DISPLAY is undefined. The items used in the Data Division as source or target for Screen Section ACCEPT or DISPLAY statements should always be non-edited fields.

Keyboard Handling Via ADIS

This section describes:

- Types of keys on the keyboard

- CRT STATUS clause

- Termination

- User function keys

- ADIS keys

- Defining in both the user and ADIS key list

- Data key handling

- ADIS-compatible GET SINGLE CHARACTER call

Function Key Handling

This section describes how to use function keys in this COBOL system. It only describes the portable method that will work on all environments. There is another method, using the x"B0" routine, which is not described here as it is machine dependent. If you are using this routine, refer to *Conflict With the x"B0" COBOL System Library Routine* later in this section for details of how this may cause problems with certain configurations.

Types of Keys on the Keyboard

In general, the keys on the keyboard can be split into two groups - data keys and function keys.

Data Keys

The data keys are those that generate characters that are in the extended ASCII character set, that is, those with ASCII codes in the range 32 to 255. During an ACCEPT operation, pressing one of these keys will simply place the character into the field. However, it is possible to disable a key completely or make it terminate the accept operation (similar to the action of a function key). This is covered later in this section.

There is a complication in that the ASCII codes in the range 0 to 31 can be considered as either data keys or function keys. For most purposes, they are treated as function keys and are disabled as data keys.

Function Keys

The most general definition of a function key is any key you would not find on a typewriter keyboard. This definition includes explicit function keys on the keyboard (usually labeled **F1, F2**, etc.) and such keys as **Escape**, the **cursor** keys, **tab**, **rubout**, etc. The return or enter key **Enter** is also treated as a function key, but with special considerations, described later.

In your COBOL system, these keys are divided into two groups - the ADIS keys and the User function keys.

ADIS Keys

This is the term given to those keys that are used by the Accept/
Display module (ADIS) during the execution of an ACCEPT
statement. This includes the **cursor** keys, **tab**, **backspace**, **delete**
and **return**.

Normally, these keys will operate as defined during an ACCEPT.
For example, the **cursor-left** key will move the cursor to the left,
backspace will erase the previous character, and so on. With the
exception of the **return** key, they will not normally terminate the
ACCEPT. However, you can make these keys terminate the
ACCEPT if required. This is described later in this section.

User Function Keys

These keys are so called because the programmer decides what
they will be used for when the application is written. There is no
predefined action assigned to these keys. The user function keys
generally include the keys labeled **F1**, **F2**, etc. and the **Escape** key
as well as any other special keys that are on the keyboard.

The CRT STATUS Clause

If you decide that you want your application to use function keys,
it is highly likely that you will want to be able to determine exactly which key has been pressed. To do this you need to include
the CRT STATUS clause in the Special-Names paragraph of your
program. For example:

```
special-names.
      crt status is key-status.
```

where key-status is a three-byte data item that should be defined
in the Working-Storage section of your program. It has the following definition:

```
01 key-status.
      03 key-type              pic x.
      03 key-code-1            pic 9(2) comp-x.
      03 key-code-2            pic 9(2) comp-x.
```

Whenever an ACCEPT statement is executed, *key-status* will be set to indicate how the ACCEPT was terminated. The exact usage of the individual fields in *key-status* is described later. However, in general they have the following uses:

key-type Indicates how the ACCEPT was terminated. The values returned are as follows :

> "0" - Normal termination of the ACCEPT
> "1" - Termination by a USER function key
> "2" - Termination by an ADIS key
> "3" - Termination by an 8 bit data key
> "4" - Termination by a 16 bit data key
> "9" - Error

These different values are described fully later in this section.

key-code-1 Indicates the number of the key that terminated the ACCEPT. The exact meaning of this number depends on the value returned in key-type.

key-code-2 If key-type and key-code-1 are zero, key-code-2 contains the raw keyboard code for the key that terminated the ACCEPT operation. Where a sequence of keystrokes rather than a single key has been configured to perform a single function, only the code for the first keystroke is returned.

If key-type is 4, key-code-2 will contain the second byte of the character which caused the ACCEPT to terminate.

Otherwise, the contents of key-code-2 are undefined.

Normal Termination of an ACCEPT

There are two cases of normal termination of an ACCEPT. They both return a value of "0" in *key-type*:

■ The most common way of terminating an ACCEPT is by pressing the return key. This will return a value of 48 (the ASCII code for "0") in *key-code-1*.

■ It is possible to configure ADIS so that an auto-skip in the last field on the screen will terminate the ACCEPT (use ADISCF to do this). This is also classed as a normal termination, but it returns a value of 1 in *key-code-1*.

Example

```
accept data-item at 0101
if key-type = "0"
      if key-code-1 = 48
            display "terminated by return key"
      else
            display "terminated by auto-skip last field"
      end-if
end-if.
```

Using the User Function Keys

There are up to 128 user function keys. Some come already configured, but you can use KEYBCF to configure the keys as needed. The defaults supplied with your COBOL system differ on different operating environments, but the following keys are standard:

PC Keystrokes	User Function Key Number
Escape	0
F1	1
F2	2
F3	3
F4	4
F5	5
F6	6
F7	7
F8	8
F9	9
F10	10

Your keyboard may not have these keys, but if they are there they should be configured as above. Additionally, on the IBM-PC family, the following user function keys are defined:

Shift+F1 - F10	11 - 20
Ctrl+F1 - F10	21 - 30
Alt+F1 - F10	31 - 40
Alt+1 - 9	41 - 49
Alt+0	50
Alt+-	51
Alt+=	52
PgUp	53
PgDn	54
Ctrl+PgUp	55
Ctrl+PgDn	56
Alt+A - Z	65 - 90

The following are available only on the extended PC keyboard.

F11	91
F12	92
Shift+F11	93
Shift+F12	94
Ctrl+F11	95
Ctrl+F12	96
Alt+F11	97
Alt+F12	98

Enabling and Disabling the User Function Keys

Before any of the user function keys can be used, they must be enabled. If a user key is enabled, it will terminate the ACCEPT operation when pressed. If the key is disabled, the key will be rejected and the bell rung.

By default, the user function keys are disabled. Micro Focus COBOL on UNIX has the user function keys enabled by default. Therefore, if you want to write programs that work in both environments, include code to enable the keys you want and disable all others.

The following call is used to selectively enable and disable the user function keys:

```
call x"af" using set-bit-pairs user-key-control
```

where:

```
01 set-bit-pairs            pic 9(2) comp-x value 1.
01 user-key-control.
     03 user-key-setting    pic 9(2) comp-x.
     03 filler              pic x value "1".
     03 first-user-key      pic 9(2) comp-x.
     03 number-of-keys      pic 9(2) comp-x.
```

The fields of user-key-control are used as follows:

user-key-setting   Set to 0 to disable keys or 1 to enable keys

first-user-key   The number of the first key to be enabled or disabled

number-of-keys   The number of consecutive keys to enable or disable

Function keys are enabled or disabled until explicitly changed by another call to x"AF" or until the application terminates. Calls to enable or disable function keys are additive. For example, if you call x"AF" to enable Function Key **F1** and then make a second call to enable **F10**, both keys are enabled.

Example

If you want to enable the Escape key and keys **F1** ... **F10**, but you want to ensure that all other user function keys are disabled, then the following code will do this:

```
* Enable 11 keys starting from key 0 (escape key)
      move 1 to user-key-setting
      move 0 to first-user-key
      move 11 to number-of-keys
      call x"af" using set-bit-pairs user-key-control
* Disable 117 keys starting from key 11
```

```
      move 0 to user-key-setting
      move 11 to first-user-key
      move 117 to number-of-keys
      call x"af" using set-bit-pairs user-key-control.
* Enable F1 and F10.
      move 1 to user-key-setting
* Enable F1.
      move 1 to first-user-key
      move 1 to number-of-keys
      call x"af" using set-bit-pairs user-key-control
* Enable F10
      move 10 to first-user-key
      call x"af" using set-bit-pairs user-key-control
```

Detecting the User Function Keys

If you press an enabled user function key during an ACCEPT operation, the ACCEPT will be terminated and the fields in *key-status* will be set as follows:

key-type	"1"
key-code-1	Set to the number of the user key that was pressed
key-code-2	Undefined

Example

```
accept data-item at 0101
if key-type = "1"
     evaluate key-code-1
            when 0 display "escape was pressed"
            when 1 display "f1 was pressed"
            when 10 display "f10 was pressed"
     end-evaluate
end-if.
```

ADIS

The User Function Keys and Validation Clauses

Normally, if a validation clause, such as FULL or REQUIRED, is specified in an ACCEPT statement, that clause must be satisfied before you can leave the field. For example, when the statement:

```
accept data-item with required
```

is executed, you will not be allowed to terminate the ACCEPT unless something has been entered into the field.

However, if an enabled user function key is pressed during an ACCEPT, it is regarded as an "exception" and will terminate the ACCEPT even if the validation clause has not been satisfied.

Using the ADIS Keys

As noted earlier, the ADIS keys are those keys that perform functions within an ACCEPT such as cursor movement, delete character, backspace, etc. However, it is possible to make these keys terminate the ACCEPT.

First, the distinction has to be made between the keys that perform the functions and the functions themselves, because there is actually a "soft" mapping between the keys and the functions they perform. This means that the programmer can change the function that one of the ADIS keys performs.

The Functions Performed by the ADIS Keys

The functions 0 to 27 are simple functions. Those in the range 55 to 62 are complex functions which may perform different actions depending on some state. For example, those functions provided for RM compatibility have a different action depending on whether or not the UPDATE clause was specified in the ACCEPT statement.

The ADIS Keys

There are 28 ADIS keys. Each of these is "mapped" onto a function, so that when a key is pressed, it performs the function it has been mapped to. What can often be confusing is that the ADIS keys themselves are given names. This name is used to distinguish the different keys, but may not necessarily describe the function the key actually performs. The following list gives the names of the keys and how to obtain them on the IBM PC keyboard.

Key Number	Key Name	Keystroke
0	Terminate accept	None
1	Terminate program	Ctrl+K
2	Carriage return	Enter
3	Cursor left	Cursor Left
4	Cursor right	Cursor Right
5	Cursor up	Cursor Up
6	Cursor down	Cursor Down
7	Home	Home
8	Tab	Tab
9	Back tab	Back tab
10	End	End
11	Next field	None
12	Previous field	None
13	Change case	Ctrl+F
14	Erase character	Backspace
15	Retype character	Ctrl+Y
16	Insert character	Ctrl+O
17	Delete character	Del
18	Restore character	Ctrl+R
19	Clear to end of field	Ctrl+Z
20	Clear field	Ctrl+X
21	Clear to end of screen	Ctrl+End
22	Clear screen	Ctrl+Home
23	Set insert mode	Ins
24	Set replace mode	None
25	Reset field	Ctrl+A
26	Start of field	None
27	Move to Mouse position	None

The keystrokes listed are the defaults shipped with your COBOL system on the IBM-PC.

Note: The carriage return (CR) key is referred to here as the
Enter key. On the IBM PC keyboard, the CR key is
labeled. On some keyboards, there is a CR key and an
Enter key. In this case, the ADIS key "Carriage Return"
should be set up as CR and the ADIS key "Terminate
Accept" should be set up as **Enter**.

Mapping the ADIS Keys to the Functions

In general, the ADIS keys are mapped onto the function of the
same name. Therefore, the **cursor-left** key will move the cursor to
the left, the **backspace** key will erase a character and so on. However, there are some keys that are by default mapped onto different functions:

Key	Function
Carriage Return	Terminate Accept (function 0)
Tab	Next Field (function 11)
Back Tab	Previous Field (function 12)
Set Insert Mode	Insert Toggle (function 58)

Therefore, when you press the **Enter** key on the IBM PC, it will
terminate the ACCEPT and when you press the **Ins** key it will
toggle between insert mode and replace mode.

At this stage, the idea of mapping keys may seem an unnecessary
complication. Where it becomes really useful is in the emulation of
other dialects of COBOL. For example, in Microsoft COBOL V2.2,
the **Enter** key moves to the next field rather than terminating the
ACCEPT. This is easy to emulate by simply changing the mapping
for key 2 (Carriage Return) from 0 (Terminate Accept) to 11 (Next
Field).

If a key is mapped on to a value of 255, that key will not perform
any function during an ACCEPT operation.

Special Mappings

All of the standard functions described above always perform the
same function, regardless of context. For example, the "Move to
next field" function will always attempt to move to the next field.

However, there are some functions that behave differently depending on the context. These functions are summarized here:

Function Number	Function Name
58	Insert Toggle
59	Replace Toggle
60	Forwards Tab
61	Backwards Tab
62	Restore

For example, the "Set Insert Mode" key (key number 23) is normally mapped to function 58 (Insert Toggle). This means that repeated pressing of the Ins key toggles between Insert and Replace mode.

Changing the Mappings from a Program

You can change the key mappings from an application program using the call:

```
call x"af" using set-map-byte adis-key-mapping
```

where:

```
01 set-map-byte                    pic 9(2) comp-x value 3.
01 adis-key-mapping.
      03 adis-mapping-byte         pic 9(2) comp-x.
      03 adis-key-number           pic 9(2) comp-x.
```

adis-key-number should be set to the number of the key you wish to change. *adis-mapping-byte* should be set to the number of the function you wish the key to be mapped to.

Example

The following code will change the action of the Backspace key (key number 14) to simply move the cursor to the left (function 3), and change the tab key (key number 8) to perform the tab function (function 8).

```
* Change mapping of cursor left key
      move 14 to adis-key-number
      move 3 to adis-mapping-byte
      call x"af" using set-map-byte adis-key-mapping
* Change mapping of the tab key
      move 8 to adis-key-number
      move 8 to adis-mapping-byte
      call x"af" using set-map-byte adis-key-mapping.
```

Conflict With X"B0" COBOL System Library Routine

The x"B0" COBOL system library routine is an alternative method of defining function keys. It is only supported on the COBOL products tailored to the IBM PC family. For further details of this call, refer to the *Library Routines* chapter. However, we recommend that you use the method of detecting function keys defined in this section rather than the X"B0" routine.

In general, you can use the x"B0" routine to define function keys which will terminate an ACCEPT. However, there is one limitation. If you use x"B0", the carriage return key must be mapped on to the "Terminate Accept" function. This is the default for this product. If you change the mapping of carriage return then any key set up by the X"B0" call will not terminate the ACCEPT. Instead, it will perform the function that carriage return has been mapped onto.

Enabling/Disabling the ADIS Keys

By default, all of the ADIS keys are enabled to perform their defined functions during an ACCEPT. However, it is possible to disable the keys or make them act as function keys instead. The call to do this is as follows:

```
call x"af" using set-bit-pairs adis-key-control
```

where:

```
01 set-bit-pairs              pic 9(2) comp-x value 1.
01 adis-key-control.
     03 adis-key-setting      pic 9(2) comp-x.
     03 filler                pic x value "2".
     03 first-adis-key        pic 9(2) comp-x.
     03 number-of-adis-keys   pic 9(2) comp-x.
```

The fields of *adis-key-control* are used as follows:

adis-key-setting	Defines the action of the keys affected, as follows:
0	The keys are disabled. If the key is pressed during an ACCEPT, the key will be rejected.
1	The key will act like a function key. If pressed during an ACCEPT, it will terminate the ACCEPT (see below).
2	The key will do its normal action during an ACCEPT (this is the default value).
3	The key will do its normal action unless it causes the cursor to leave the current field. If this happens, it will act like a function key.
first-adis-key	The number of the first key to be affected.
number-of-adis-keys	The number of consecutive keys to be affected.

Detection of ADIS Keys

If an ADIS key has been set up to act as a function key, it will terminate the ACCEPT operation and key-status will be set up with the following values.

key-type	"2"
key-code-1	Set to the number of the ADIS key that was pressed. Note that this is the number of the

key not the number of the function the key
has been mapped to.

key-code-2 Undefined.

Example

The following code sets up Tab and Backtab to act as function
keys and the cursor left and cursor right keys to act as function
keys if they cause the cursor to leave the field.

```
* Set up tab (key 8) and back-tab (Key 9) to act as
* function keys
      move 1 to adis-key-setting
      move 8 to first-adis-key
      move 2 to number-of-adis-keys
      call x"af" using set-bit-pairs adis-key-control
* Set up cursor left (key 3) and cursor right (key 4)
* to act as function keys ONLY if they cause the cursor
* to leave the field.
      move 3 to adis-key-setting
      move 3 to first-adis-key
      move 2 to number-of-adis-keys
      call x"af" using set-bit-pairs adis-key-control
      accept data-item at 0101

      if key-type = "2"
        evaluate key-code-1
          when 3
              display "cursor left caused the cursor to
-            "leave the field"
          when 4
              display "cursor right caused thecursor to
-            "leave the field"
          when 8
              display "the tab key was pressed"
          when 9
              display "the back tab key was pressed"
        end-evaluate
end-if.
```

Data Key Handling

The data keys are the 256 keys in the extended ASCII character set. Normally, when you press one of these keys during an AC-CEPT, the character is simply put straight into the field. The exception to this is the keys with ASCII codes in the range 0 to 31, that is, the control keys. These are generally disabled.

Controlling the Data Keys

Just like most other keys on the keyboard, it is possible to disable data keys or make them act like function keys, that is, terminate the ACCEPT. To do this, use the following call:

```
call x"af" using set-bit-pairs data-key-control
```

where:

```
01 set-bit-pairs           pic 9(2) comp-x value 1.
01 data-key-control.
     03 data-key-setting     pic 9(2) comp-x.
     03 filler               pic x value "3".
     03 first-data-key       pic x.
     03 number-of-data-keys  pic 9(2) comp-x.
```

The fields in *data-key-control* should be set up as follows:

data-key-setting	Defines the action of the keys affected, as follows:
0	The key is disabled. If it is pressed, during an ACCEPT, the bell is rung and the key rejected.
1	The key will act as a function key (see below). It will terminate the ACCEPT.
2	(The default.) The character will simply be entered into the field.
first-data-key	The first character to be affected.

number-of-data-keys	The number of characters to be affected.

Detecting Data Keys Set Up to Act as Function Keys

If a data key has been set up to act as a function key, it will terminate the ACCEPT when pressed and *key-status* will be set up as follows:

key-type	"3"
key-code-1	Set to the ASCII code of the key that was pressed
key-code-2	Undefined

Example

```
* Set up the characters "A" to "Z" to terminate the
* ACCEPT
     move 1 to data-key-setting
     move "a" to first-data-key
     move 26 to number-of-data-keys
     call x"af" using set-bit-pairs data-key-control
     accept data-item at 0101
     if key-type = "3"
         evaluate key-code-1
            when 65
              display "a pressed"
            when 66
              display "b pressed"
            when 90
              display "z pressed"
         end-evaluate
     end-if.
```

Get Single Character Routine

This routine allows you to get a single key from the keyboard. It uses ADIS itself, so all of the function keys supported by ADIS are supported. The routine only reads the keyboard and so does not echo the key to the screen.

The format of the call is:

```
call x"af" using get-single-char-func key-status
```

where:

```
01 get-single-char-func          pic 9(2) comp-x value 26.

01 key-status.
      03 key-type                pic x.
      03 key-code.
            05 key-code-1         pic 9(2) comp-x.
            05 key-code-2         pic 9(2) comp-x.
```

The values returned in *key-status* are the same as those described previously, except that a value of "0" is never returned in *key-type* by this call. The carriage return key returns a value of "2" in *key-type* and a value of 2 in *key-code-1*.

The values returned in key-status are as follows:

key-type **key-code-1**

"1"   Returns the number of the user function pressed.

"2"   Returns the number of the ADIS key pressed. Note that no mapping of keys occurs in this call. Therefore the number returned is the number of the actual key pressed.

"3"   Returns the ASCII code of the 8 bit data key pressed.

"4"   Returns the first byte of the 16 bit data key pressed. The second byte is contained in *key-code-2*. Only applicable on machines that support double-byte characters.

"9"   Error condition. Values are:

8   Disabled character. The data key pressed is disabled.

9   Invalid keystroke. A function key has been
pressed that is not defined in either the user
or ADIS function key list.

Example

```
call x"af" using get-single-char-func key-status
evaluate key-type
    when "1"
*        User function key pressed. Do required
*        action depending on value in key-code-1.
    when "2"
*        ADIS function key pressed. Do required
*        action depending on value in key-code-1.
    when "3"
*        Data key pressed. Do required action
         depending on the ASCII code in key-code-1.
    when "4"
*        Double byte data key pressed. Do required
*        action depending on the 16-bit character in
*        key-code.
    when "9"
*        Invalid or disabled key. Do required action.
end-evaluate.
```

Program Sample

```
****************************************************
* This program is an example of how to write
* programs that make use of function keys.
*
* It is assumed that the Escape key is available,
* but any other function key can be selected by
* either pressing the function key or by pressing
* "/" followed by the first letter of the option.
*
* This program assumes that the Default
* Configuration has been selected using ADISCF.
****************************************************
```

```
special-names.
    cursor is cursor-position
    crt status is key-status.

data division.
working-storage section.

***************************************************
* Parameters to be used for the X"AF" calls.
***************************************************

01 set-bit-pairs              pic 9(2) comp-x value 1.
01 get-single-character       pic 9(2) comp-x value 26.

01 enable-esc-and-f1.
    03 filler                 pic 9(2) comp-x value 1.
    03 filler                 pic x value "1".
    03 filler                 pic 9(2) comp-x value 0.
    03 filler                 pic 9(2) comp-x value 2.

01 disable-all-other-user-keys.
    03 filler                 pic 9(2) comp-x value 0.
    03 filler                 pic x value "1".
    03 filler                 pic 9(2) comp-x value 2.
    03 filler                 pic 9(2) comp-x value 126.

01 enable-slash-key.
    03 filler                 pic 9(2) comp-x value 1.
    03 filler                 pic x value "3".
    03 filler                 pic x value "/".
    03 filler                 pic 9(2) comp-x value 1.


***************************************************
* Status returned after termination of an ACCEPT.
***************************************************

01 key-status.
    03 key-type               pic x.
    03 key-code-1             pic 9(2) comp-x.
    03 key-code-1-x           redefines key-code-1 pic x.
    03 key-code-2             pic 9(2) comp-x.
```

```
****************************************************
* Cursor-Position is returned by ADIS containing
* the psition of the cursor when the ACCEPT was
* terminated.
****************************************************


01 cursor-position.
      03 cursor-row              pic 99.
      03 cursor-column           pic 99.


****************************************************
* Work Areas used by the program.
****************************************************


01 work-areas.
      03 wa-name                 pic x(30).
      03 wa-address-line-1       pic x(40).
      03 wa-address-line-2       pic x(40).
      03 wa-address-line-3       pic x(40).
      03 wa-address-line-4       pic x(40).
      03 wa-age                  pic 999.

01 exit-flag                     pic 9(2) comp-x value 0.


****************************************************
* Screen Section.
****************************************************
screen section.


01 main-screen.
     03 blank screen.
     03 line 2 column 27
         value "typical data entry screen".
     03 line 3 column 27
         value "——————————".
     03 line 5 column 1 value "name        [".
     03 pic x(30) using wa-name highlight prompt " ".
     03 value "]".
     03 line 7 column 1 value "address    [".
     03 pic x(40) using wa-address-line-1 highlight prompt " ".
     03 value "]".
     03 line 8 column 1 value "              [".
     03 pic x(40) using wa-address-line-2 highlight prompt " ".
     03 value "]".
```

```
      03 line 9 column 1 value "          [".
      03 pic x(40) using wa-address-line-3 highlight prompt " ".
      03 value "]".
      03 line 10 column 1 value "          [".
      03 pic x(40) using wa-address-line-4 highlight prompt " ".
      03 value "]".
      03 line 12 column 1 value "age        [".
      03 pic zz9 using wa-age highlight prompt " ".
      03 value "]".
      03 line 20 column 1 value
         "_____
-        "_____".
      03 line 21 column 1 value "f1" highlight.
      03 value "=/help".
      03 column 75 value "esc" highlight.
      03 value "ape".


01 help-screen.
      03 blank screen.
      03 line 1 column 34 value "help screen".
      03 line + 1 column 34 value "————".
      03 line 4 value "escape" highlight.
      03 value "      leave this program.".
      03 line 6 column 1 value "f1 or /h" highlight.
      03 value "   obtains this screen.".
      03 line 8 column 1
         value "use cursor keys to move around ".
      03 value "the fields on the screen".
      03  value "enter will".
      03 line + 1 column 1 value "accept the data ".
      03  value " present new blank form to fill in.".
      03 line 24 column 25
         value "press any key to continue ...".


****************************************************
* Procedure Division.
****************************************************
procedure division.
entry-point section.


* First we want to ensure that the keys are enabled as we want
* them. Enable the Escape and F1 keys.
```

```
          call x"af" using set-bit-pairs
                          enable-esc-and-f1
```

* disable every other user function key.

```
          call x"af" using
               set-bit-pairs disable-all-other-user-keys
```

* set up "/" key to act as a function key and terminate
* the accept.

```
          call x"af" using set-bit-pairs
                          enable-slash-key
```

* Now ensure that the cursor position will be returned when an
* ACCEPT is terminated. Setting to row 1, column 1 will ensure
* that the cursor will be initially positioned at the start of
* the first field.

```
          move 1 to cursor-row
          move 1 to cursor-column
```

* Loop until the Escape key is pressed.

```
          perform until exit-flag = 1
               display main-screen
               accept main-screen
               evaluate key-type
               when "0"
```

* Accept terminated normally, i.e., the Enter key was pressed.
* Here, we simply blank out the work areas and restart in the
* first field.

```
               move spaces to work-areas
               move 1 to cursor-row
               move 1 to cursor-column

               when "1"
```

* A user function key has been pressed. This will either be
* Esc or F1 as all others have been disabled.

```
                          if key-code-1 = 0
```

* Escape has been pressed, so we wish to leave the program.

```
                          move 1 to exit-flag
                   else
```

* F1 has been pressed so display the help screen.

```
                          perform display-help-screen
                   end-if

               when "3"
```

* A data key has terminated the Accept. It must be "/" as no
* other keys have been enabled to do this. Now get the next
* character to see if "H" or "h" has been pressed.

```
                   call x"af" using
                        get-single-character key-status
                   if key-type = "3" and
                        (key-code-1-x = "h" or
                        key-code-1-x = "h")
                      perform display-help-screen
                   end-if

            end-evaluate
        end-perform
        stop run.

display-help-screen section.
```

* Display the help screen and then wait for a key to be
pressed.

```
        display help-screen
        call x"af" using
             get-single-character key-status.
```

Mouse Handling Via ADIS

This section descibes how to use a mouse with COBOL programs that use ADIS to handle the scree and keyboard. It shows you how to activate the mouse, and use it in the ADIS ACCEPT.

Using the Mouse

This section describes how to access the mouse for use in screen handling in this COBOL system. By default the mouse is not active so the routines below must be called to allow the mouse to be used. The mouse is only available if the relevant mouse drivers, supplied with the mouse or the operating system, are installed.

Having the mouse pointer enabled during an ADIS ACCEPT statement alows your user to alter the current input field by moving the mouse pointer over another field and pressing the leftmost button on the mouse. This will result in the text cursor being moved to the mouse pointer position.

The leftmost button on the mouse is treated as ADIS key number 27 and bhaves in the same way as all other ADIS keys. The example t the end of this section shows how the action of the leftmost button can be changed so the mouse can be used to terminate an accept operation.

Once the mouse is active (and enabled) the mouse cursor will move on the screen when the mouse is moved. This happens independently of any ADIS operations. ADIS wll take notice of the mouse only when a mouse button is pressed. However the program can determine the position of the mouse at any time using the appropriate routine described below.

Activating/Terminating Use of a Mouse

You control whether a mouse driver is in use or not as follows:

```
call x"af" using use-mouse-function
                 usage-parameter
```

where:

```
01 use-mouse-function        pic 9(2) comp-x value 64.
01 usage-parameter           pic 9(2) comp-x.
```

usage-parameter should be set as follows:

0   Terminate the mouse. The mouse pointer is deleted and no further mouse action is possible.

1   Activate the mouse. This activates the mouse driver and draws the mouse pointer.

On return, use-mouse-function contains 255 if no mouse is present.

Example

The following code will activate the mouse:

```
move 1 to usage-parameter
call x"af" using use-mouse-function
              usage-parameter
```

Enabling/Disabling the Mouse

You disable or re-enable the mouse as follows:

```
call x"af" using enable-mouse-function
                 enable-parameter
```

where:

```
01 enable-mouse-function     pic 9(2) comp-x value 66.
01 enable-parameter          pic 9(2) comp-x.
```

enable-parameter should be set as follows:

0   Disable the mouse. The mouse pointer is hidden and all mouse movement and button presses are ignored until the mouse is reactivated.

1   Re-enable the mouse. This redraws the mouse pointer, that is, makes it visible, and re-enables the ability to detect mouse movement and button presses.

Example

The following code will disable the mouse:

```
move 0 to enable-parameter
call x"af" using enable-mouse-function
                 enable-parameter
```

Returning Mouse Status and Position

You get the position of the mouse pointer and the status of the mouse driver as follows:

```
call x"af" using get-mouse-details
                 mouse-details
```

where:

```
01 get-mouse-details          pic 9(2) comp-x value 67.
01 mouse-details.
    03 mouse-x-position       pic 9(4) comp-x.
    03 mouse-y-position       pic 9(4) comp-x.
    03 mouse-status           pic 9(4) comp-x.
```

The status value returned is as defined for the *event-type* field of the low-level mouse routines in the chapter *Library Routines (Call-by-Name)*.

Example

The following code will display the mouse pointer position:

```
call x"af" using get-mouse-details mouse-details
display "mouse-x-position is" at line 1 column 1
```

```
display mouse-x-position at line 1 column 22
display "mouse-y-position is"at line 2 column 1
display mouse-y-position at line 2 column 22
```

Example of Using a Mouse

The following code sets up the mouse to act as a function key. Pressing the left-hand mouse button will terminate the ACCEPT operation and cause the mouse coordinates to be displayed. The data items are as defined in the details of the routines above.

```
* Activate the mouse
    move 1 to usage-parameter
    call x"af" using use-mouse-function
                usage-parameter
* Set the mouse (key 27) to act as a function key
    move 3 to adis-key-setting
    move 27 to first-adis-key
    move 2 to number-of-adis-keys
    call x"af" using set-bit-pairs
                    adis-key-control
    accept data-item at 0101
    if key-type = "2" and key-code-1 = 27
            display "the mouse terminated the accept"
            call x"af" using get-mouse-details
                            mouse-details
            display "mouse-x-position is " at line 3 column 1
            display mouse-x-position at line 3 column 22
            display "mouse-y-position is " at line 4 column 1
            display mouse-y-position at line 4 column 22
    end-if
* Terminate the mouse
    move 1 to usage-parameter
    call x"af" using use-mouse-function
                usage-parameter
```

Chapter 4

COBOL File Handling

One of the many benefits COBOL has to offer as a language is its built-in data file handling capabilities. COBOL uses simple syntax to achieve powerful management of sequential, relative and indexed sequential files.

Overview

This chapter provides information on file handling in Personal COBOL, and relates COBOL file handling to the way files are handled by the operating system. The chapter covers the following topics:

- COBOL data file organizations

- COBOL file naming conventions

- file name extensions used in Personal COBOL

File Handling

COBOL File Handling

COBOL Data File Organizations

MERANT Micro Focus COBOL supports four different types of file organization:
SEQUENTIAL
LINE SEQUENTIAL
RELATIVE
INDEXED.

A data file's organization is defined in the SELECT statement of a program's Input Output Section, by using the phrase

```
ORGANIZATION IS XXXX
```
where XXXX is one of the four types, e.g. RELATIVE.

It's important to note, that if the organization of a file is not defined in the SELECT statement, the system normally defaults to treating the file organization as SEQUENTIAL and of course, this leads to data errors if the file is actually a different organization such as a text file.

NOTE: the descriptions below cover fixed-length record files only. These are the default. Variable-length record files also have a more complicated structure, which is not dealt with here. Special syntax is used to create and handle variable-length record files.

I. SEQUENTIAL organization

Sequential files are the simplest form of COBOL data file. Records are placed in the file in the order they are written, and can only be read back in the same order.

This is the default organization -if the organization is not specified in the SELECT statement then the file will default to ORGANIZATION SEQUENTIAL. In MERANT COBOL this organization is also called RECORD SEQUENTIAL, to show that it is different from LINE SEQUENTIAL.

When a record of a RECORD SEQUENTIAL file is written, all the data in the record area defined in the FD is written to disk with nothing added or removed. Unlike LINE SEQUENTIAL records (which are described below), trailing spaces are not removed and no record termination bytes are added. In the file on disk the records follow each other with nothing in between. Thus, if a text file is read as a SEQUENTIAL file (i.e. without using the phrase ORGANIZATION LINE SEQUENTIAL in the SELECT statement), the carriage return and line feed characters will be read as normal data. They will show up in the program as a musical note and a small circle, and they will push the 'real' valid data out of its correct position in the record.

II. LINE SEQUENTIAL organization

LINE SEQUENTIAL files are a special type of SEQUENTIAL file. They have sequential records, which can be accessed only in the order they were written, but the records vary in length and each ends with a carriage-return and line-feed.

Text files produced by most regular editors, like the Personal COBOL editors, are LINE SEQUENTIAL files. So if you want a COBOL program to read or write a text file you must add the phrase ORGANIZATION LINE SEQUENTIAL to the SELECT statement. The statement might read, for example:

```
SELECT MY-TEXT-FILE
ASSIGN TO "AUTHORS.TXT"
ORGANIZATION LINE SEQUENTIAL.
```

In Text files on disk, each record in the file has two "terminator bytes" separating it from the next record. These bytes are a carriage return (x"0D") and a line feed (x"0A") character. For a file defined as LINE SEQUENTIAL, the Personal COBOL system removes the termination bytes when a record is read from disk; they do not appear in your program. The system also adds the termination bytes automatically when a LINE SEQUENTIAL record is written to disk. Similarly when a text (line sequential) record is written, any spaces at the end of the record are removed by the system. When a text record is read, if the data is shorter than the number of characters in the FD then spaces are added to the data to fill the record.

In a "record sequential" file the system will read exactly the number of characters defined in the FD; in a "line sequential" file the system will read the lesser of the number of characters up to the first carriage-return/line-feed pair, or the number of characters defined in the FD.

The COBOL system can be told default to LINE SEQUENTIAL instead of RECORD SEQUENTIAL, to handle text data files, without modifying the program source code. Use the compiler directive SEQUENTIAL"LINE" -which tells the compiler that the default for all sequential files in a program is text format. When this directive is used, if any sequential files are NOT text then they must be indicated to the system by adding ORGANIZATION IS RECORD SEQUENTIAL to the SELECT statement.

Compiler directives are documented in the online Help under Standard COBOL Reference.

File Handling

III.RELATIVE organization

Every record in a relative file can be accessed directly without having to read
through any other records. A unique ordinal number when it is written and when it
is read back identify each record. The identifier is defined in working-storage and
declared in the SELECT statement:

```
SELECT MY-RELATIVE-FILE
ASSIGN TO "WIDGETS.DAT"
ORGANIZATION RELATIVE
ACCESS RANDOM
RELATIVE REL-NUM.
. . .
WORKING-STORAGE SECTION.
01 REL-NUM    PIC 9(8).
. . .
MOVE 12345 TO REL-NUM
READ MY-RELATIVE-FILE
```

IV. INDEXED organization

Indexed files are the most complex form of COBOL file handled directly by the
syntax of this COBOL system. A unique user-defined key identifies records in an
indexed file when written. Each record can contain any number of user-defined
keys, which can be used to read the record, either directly or in key sequence.

```
SELECT IFILE ASSIGN "LANG.DAT"
ORGANIZATION INDEXED
ACCESS RANDOM
RECORD KEY IREC-INDEX.

FD IFILE.
01 IREC.
    03 IREC-INDEX          PIC X(10).
    03 IREC-DATA           PIC X(20).

MOVE "COBOL" TO IREC-INDEX
READ IFILE
```

Both RELATIVE and INDEXED files have a more complex internal arrangement than
SEQUENTIAL or LINE SEQUENTIAL files. The system adds extra data to the disk file
so it can locate records appropriately. In general RELATIVE or INDEXED files are
best handled using COBOL syntax, and are difficult to handle any other way. If REL-
ATIVE or INDEXED files are shown on the screen, using DOS's TYPE command for
example, they will not show their contents properly, because of the extra data.

Indexed files in this COBOL system are written and read as two physical files. One file contains the data, and one file contains the index. The index part is always named with the same file name as the data, with the extension IDX. Thus the file called LANG.DAT in the example above has an index called LANG.IDX.

COBOL File Naming Conventions

The name of a file used in a program is often different from the name used in the operating system; the name chosen are entirely up to the programmer. Data file assignment lets you tie the logical files of a program (that is, the file names as used internally by the program) to physical disk files (i.e. the names as used by the operating system). The physical name you supply can include a drive name and/or a path; if the physical name does not include a drive or path then the system assumes the file is in the current directory.

A data file's name is assigned by the ASSIGN clause in the SELECT statement of the FILE-CONTROL paragraph of the ENVIRONMENT DIVISION. The record layout is defined in the File Description (FD) entry in the FILE SECTION of the DATA DIVISION.

IMPORTANT NOTE: If no physical file name is defined in an assignment clause the COBOL system automatically supplies a physical name based on the logical file name, which might not be a valid name for the operating system.

The Personal COBOL system provides three types of file assignment:

I. Fixed File Assignment,

The logical filename is assigned to a literal filename (a name explicitly defined inside quotes, like "C:\MYFILE.DAT") at the time you write your program. This file name cannot be changed without recompiling your program.

Example 1a Fixed File Assignment, type a
The file name is defined in the select statement as a literal. In this example the name of the file on disk will be MYFIL1A.DAT:

```
      SELECT MYFIL1A ASSIGN "AFILE.DAT".
      • • •
      OPEN MYFILE1A
```

Example 1b Fixed File Assignment, type b
The file's name is defined in a somewhat vague way that can be confusing. The compiler automatically allocates a physical file name the same as the logical file name. In this case the DOS file will be called "MYFIL1B". The physical name allocated by the compiler is based on the logical name, so it is possible to get an "illegal file name" message if the logical filename includes letters which are invalid in DOS file names.

```
SELECT MYFIL1B ASSIGN TO DISK.
. . .
OPEN MYFILE1B
```

II. Dynamic File Assignment

The logical name is assigned to a data item defined in your program. You store the name of the physical file in the data item at run time before opening the file. You can choose to define the data item explicitly in the Data Division. If you do not then the COBOL system supplies an implicit definition of PIC X(65).

In either case, you must move a valid file name into the data item before using it in an OPEN statement. This method allows a single file definition to be used to access any number of physical files in one program.

Example 2a Dynamic File Assignment, type a
The filename is going to be defined in the working storage item 'myfil2a-name'. A valid DOS filename is required in the data item when the file OPEN statement is executed. E.g.:

```
SELECT MYFIL2A ASSIGN MYFIL2A-NAME.
. . .
05 MYFILE2A-NAME PIC X(20).
. . .
MOVE "ABC.DAT" to MYFILE2A-NAME
OPEN MYFILE2A
. . .
CLOSE MYFILE2A
MOVE "XYZ.DAT" to MYFILE2A-NAME
OPEN MYFILE2A
. . . etc.
```

Example 2b Dynamic File Assignment, type b
The data item for the filename is not defined in the Data Division, but will be automatically defined by the compiler. A valid DOS filename is required in the data item when the file OPEN statement is executed. Note that this example does not define MYFILE2B-NAME anywhere, so it is allocated as PIC X(65) by the compiler.

```
SELECT MYFIL2B ASSIGN MYFIL2B-NAME.
. . .
MOVE "MYFILE2B.DAT" to MYFILE2B-NAME
OPEN MYFILE2B
```

File Handling

III. External File Assignment

The ASSIGN clause names an environment variable in the operating system. The environment variable must be set in the operating system, usually before the program is executed, to define a valid filename before the file is opened. In DOS you can do this by typing SET envvar=afile at the DOS command prompt (using any valid environment variable name for 'envvar' and any valid DOS filename for 'afile'). See your operating system manual for details of how to set environment variables.

This method allows flexibility in use of a program in different situations, where file names can be changed without altering the program varying pathnames from one machine to another for example.

Example 3 External File Assignment
The following SELECT assigns the logical file MYFIL3 to the operating system environment variable MYFIL3NAME. A valid filename is required in the environment variable when the file OPEN statement is executed:

```
SELECT MYFIL3 ASSIGN EXTERNAL MYFIL3NAME.
```

Filename extensions used in this COBOL system

The COBOL system uses file name extensions to identify what a file contains. For example, the editor and compiler assume that files with the extension CBL contain COBOL source code. The system will create files, which have the same base name as your program, but will have a different extension. When a program with the name MYPROG.CBL is compiled, MYPROG.INT and MYPROG.IDY will be created, and perhaps several other files also, with different file name extensions.

The following list describes many of the file name extensions used by the COBOL system. We recommend caution when these extensions are used for names of other files.

ASV	auto-save from an edit session
BAK	backup copy of source code
BIN	a binary executable
CBL	COBOL source code
CFG	configuration text file
CLS	OO class information
CPB	COBOL copybook (source) files
CPY	ditto
CSI	source information also used by Animator
DLE	dynamic-load executable
DLW	dynamic-load executable
DOC	ordinary text (ASCII -not Word format)
EVT	OO definition
EXE	executable file (not produced by Personal COBOL)
GS	Dialog System screen set
HLP	Windows format online help
HNF	Micro Focus format online help
ICN	icon
IDX	index part of indexed file (this extension must not be used in the user's filename)
IDY	debugger info from the compiler used by Animator2
IF	OO definition
ILS	Animator query data
INI	initialization text file
INS	OO definition
INT	intermediate (compiled) code
LBR	COBOL Library
LST	compiled source listing
MSG	error message list
SRN	screen definition form
SS	screen section copy file
PRJ	project file (used by the OO Browser)
WKS	Screen definition working storage

File Handling

File Handling

Chapter 5

Compiler Directives

This chapter lists and describes the directives you can use to control the Personal COBOL compiler. Directives are used to specify options that affect the way the compiler behaves, what output it produces and how the compiled code behaves when run. All directives have a default built into the compiler; however, you can create your own defaults as described in *Setting Directives* below.

Setting Directives

Directives, which are specified prior to compiling, can be entered in a number of ways, and the order in which various options are passed to the compiler determines their precedence. At startup the compiler processes directives in the following sequence:

1. Directives are read from the file COBOL.DIR (if present), which is automatically processed every time you use the compiler.
2. Directives from the check menu **F9/F10=directives** option.
3. Directives from $SET statements in the program source code.

The setting of directives in COBOL.DIR, the check menu **F9/F10=directives** option, or $SET statements override their default settings. Additionally, later settings override earlier ones. So for example, specifying NOLIST in a $SET statement will override LIST() in COBOL.DIR.

The COBOL.DIR Directives File

COBOL.DIR is a directives file which is processed automatically by the compiler. Consequently, directives contained in COBOL.DIR override the defaults built into the compiler. The directives file is a standard ASCII text file containing any number of lines. Each line may contain one or more directives or comments. Directives in the directives file must be separated by a space and cannot be broken across two lines. Comment lines are indicated by an ampersand character (&) in column 1.

The compiler will look for a COBOL.DIR file first in the current directory. If it finds one there it will use it. Otherwise it will look in the COBOL system directories indicated by the environment variable COBDIR.

If the compiler rejects directives in the COBOL.DIR file compilation will continue. Therefore, if you create a COBOL.DIR file you should do a trial compilation and watch for "Rejected" messages at the beginning when the directives are being processed. If any occur, correct the COBOL.DIR file and retry until no errors are reported.

The $SET Statement

Many directives can be specified in the program source code in $SET statements. You specify the $SET statement in the following format with the $ character in column 7.

```
$set <directive> . . .
```

where <directive> is one or more of the compiler directives.

If more than one directive is specified, then they must be separated by spaces. A $SET statement cannot be continued onto a new line, but it can be followed by additional $SET statements.

An "initial" $SET statement is one that is not preceded in the source file by any other source statements except other $SET statements. When a directive is specified on a $SET other than an initial $SET, it affects compilation from the point the $SET is encountered onwards. The List of Directives below indicates which directives are allowed on $SET statements, distinguishing those only allowed on initial $SET statements.

List of Directives

COPYLIST	List COPY files
CURRENCY-SIGN	PIC currency sign
CURRENT-DATE	MMDDYY OR DDMMYY
DATE	Date for listings
ERRLIST	Print messages only
FORM	Page length
LIST	File for listing
LW	Page width
MF	Enable MF extensions
NESTCALL	Allow nested progs
OPTIONAL-FILE	All files optional
OVERRIDE	Change reserved word
REF	Addresses in listings
REMOVE	De-reserve a word
RESEQ	Generate line numbers
SEQCHK	Check line numbers
SEQUENTIAL	Specifies default file type
SIGN	Sign convention either ASCII or EBCDIC
TIME	Put time on listings
WARNING	Message output level
XREF	Produce cross-ref

Descriptions of Directives

COPYLIST

Makes the compiler list the contents of files named in COPY statements.

Syntax:

Compiler Directives

Parameters:

integer   Must be between 0 and 99. The segment-number

Default: COPYLIST

$SET: Any

The segment-number is the number of a COBOL segment. It must be in the range 50 through 99. If it is not specified, the contents of all COPY-files are listed. If it is specified, the contents of all COPY-files in the first three divisions (that is, the Identification, Environment and Data Divisions), the root, and the given segment are listed. An integer of 0 refers to the first three divisions and all root segments.

NOCOPYLIST prevents the listing of the contents of any COPY-files. If a segment-number is specified with NOCOPYLIST, only COPY-files in that segment are listed. For example:

COPYLIST"53"   List all COPY-files in the first three divisions, the root segment, and segment 53.

NO COPYLIST"53"   List only COPY-files that are in segment 53.

Whatever the state of this directive, the name of any COPY-file open when a page heading is output is given in that heading.

CURRENCY-SIGN

Specifies the currency sign to be recognized in the PICTURE clause.

Syntax:

Parameters:

integer   ASCII code of the character, in decimal.

Default:	CURRENCY-SIGN "36" (that is, "$")
$SET:	Initial

You cannot specify a symbol which is also a valid PICTURE clause symbol.

CURRENT-DATE

Specifies the format of the date stored in the CURRENT-DATE special register.

Syntax:

Parameters:

date-format	Either DDMMYY or YYMMDD.
Default:	CURRENT-DATE "MMDDYY"
$SET:	Any

The DDMMYY parameter causes CURRENT-DATE to be stored in European format. The parameter can be specified in either upper-case or lower-case.

DATE

Puts the date in the DATE-COMPILED paragraph and at the top of each page of the listing.

Syntax:

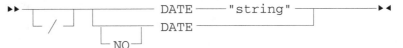

Parameters:

string   An alphanumeric literal.

Default: DATE

$SET: No

Your personal computer keeps the date and time in the operating system. They are automatically inserted when you specify DATE. You can, however, enter the date yourself as the parameter. With NODATE, the paragraph is left unaltered.

With DATE, the system date or the string you enter appears at the top of each page of the listing. With NODATE, spaces are used instead.

ERRLIST

Specifies that the listing is to contain no source lines except those that have errors or flags.

Syntax:

Parameters: None

Default: NOERRLIST

$SET: No

FORM

Specifies the number of lines on each page of the listing.

Syntax:

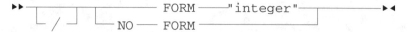

Parameters:

integer   Must be greater than 3.

Default: FORM"60"

$SET: Any

With FORM, a form-feed character is always produced at the head of the listing file. With NOFORM, no form-feed characters or page headings are produced anywhere in the listing.

LIST

Specifies the destination of the source listing file.

Syntax:

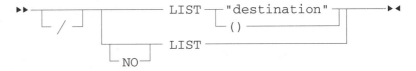

Parameters:

destination   A full file specification or a device-name.

Default: LIST

$SET: Any

If you specify an existing file, it is overwritten. When NOLIST is specified, no source listing is produced. If you specify LIST with no destination, the source listing is sent to the screen.

The device-name can be any suitable device, such as CON: for the screen. LIST and NOLIST with no parameter may be used in $SET statements within a program to list selected parts of the program. The destination of the listing cannot be changed in this way.

LIST() causes the source listing to be put in the file source-filename.LST, where source-filename is the root of the name of the program being compiled. Note that with this parameter you must use parentheses not quotes.

If you want to list the source to a file for every compilation you do, place the LIST() directive in the COBOL.DIR file. This will override the default LIST.

Alternatively, if you already have a LIST directive in your COBOL.DIR, making every listing go to the screen, you can override it by using LIST() on the command line.

LW

Sets the width of the listing.

Syntax:

Parameters:

integer	Width in characters. It must be between 72 and 132.
Default:	LISTWIDTH"72"
$SET:	Any

LW"132" causes additional information to be displayed for each line listed. This includes the first eight characters of the current copy file name (spaces for the main file) together with the number of the line relative to the start of that file.

MF

Facilitates forward compatibility with Micro Focus products by selectively enabling Micro Focus-specific reserved words and changing the behavior of certain features to be compatible with particular versions.

Syntax:

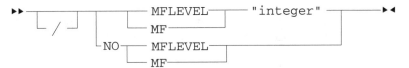

Parameters:

integer   The level of Micro Focus COBOL to be compatible with.

Default: MF"7"

$SET: Initial

The possible values of the parameter are:

7   COBOL/2 v2.5
     COBOL/2 Workbench v2.5
     Personal COBOL 2.0

If you specify MF without the parameter, all Micro Focus specific reserved words are treated as reserved words. It is equivalent to specifying MF"7". If you specify NOMF, none of the Micro Focus reserved words are treated as reserved words.

NESTCALL

Enables compilation of nested programs.

Syntax:

Parameters: None

Default: NONESTCALL

$SET: Initial

OPTIONAL-FILE

Makes the compiler treat all files opened for I-O or EXTEND as optional.

Syntax:

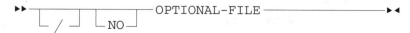

Parameters: None

Default: OPTIONAL-FILE

$SET: Initial

Under ANSI'85 Standard COBOL, a file is treated as optional only if it has the OPTIONAL phrase in its SELECT statement. For compatibility with the ANSI'85 Standard you must specify the NO OPTIONAL-FILE directive.

OVERRIDE

Replaces a reserved word by a new one.

Syntax:

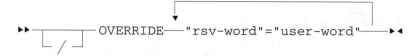

Parameters:

rsv-word   Existing reserved-word.

user-word   Any COBOL word not the same as an existing reserved word.

Default: No change of reserved words takes place.

$SET: Initial

This directive equates an existing reserved-word to the specified user-defined-word, so that, in the program, user-defined-word will be treated as a reserved word, and reserved-word will be treated as a user-defined word.

The equals sign must be surrounded by spaces. If the parameters are repeated they must be separated by spaces.

REF

Makes the compiler include in the source listing the intermediate code address of each data item or Procedure Division statement; and in the object code listing, the address of each Procedure Division statement.

Syntax:

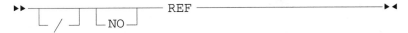

Parameters: None

Default: NOREF

$SET: Any

The address is 4 digits long and appears on the right-hand side.

This directive needs a line width setting of at least 90 (Specify the directive LW"90").

This directive can be useful in determining the locations reported in run-time error messages.

This directive can be enabled by the Personal COBOL check menu **F7=ref** switch. Press the **F7** key until the word REF appears on the information line. This automatically also enables LW(90).

REMOVE

Removes words from the reserved word list, so that they can be used as user-defined words.

Syntax:

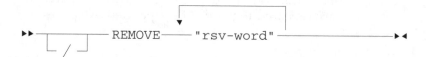

Parameters:

rsv-word   A reserved word.

Default: No reserved words are removed.

$SET: Initial

RESEQ

Makes the compiler produce line numbers.

Syntax:

Parameters: None

Default: RESEQ

$SET: Initial

These are COBOL line sequence numbers, starting at 1 and increasing in increments of 1.

SEQCHK

Makes the compiler check the sequence numbers in columns 1 through 6 and identify source lines that are out of sequence.

Syntax:

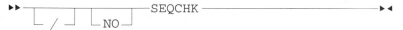

Parameters:	None
Default:	NOSEQCHK
$SET:	Any

SEQUENTIAL

Specifies the default file type for files defined (implicitly or explicitly) as ORGANIZATION SEQUENTIAL.

Syntax:

![SEQUENTIAL—"type" syntax diagram]

Parameters: type   ADVANCING, ANSI, LINE, or RECORD.

Properties:
Default: SEQUENTIAL"RECORD"
Phase: Syntax check
Environment: All
$SET: Initial

Dependencies: Set to SEQUENTIAL"RECORD" immediately by NORM or RM"ANSI".
Set to SEQUENTIAL"LINE" immediately by RM.

Comments: The possible values of *type* are:

ADVANCING	RECORD SEQUENTIAL with LINE ADVANCING.
ANSI	ANSI-conforming RECORD SEQUENTIAL.
LINE	LINE SEQUENTIAL.
RECORD	RECORD SEQUENTIAL (a standard SEQUENTIAL file).

SIGN

Specifies whether, for numeric DISPLAY items with included signs, the signs are to be interpreted according to the ASCII or EBCDIC convention.

Syntax:

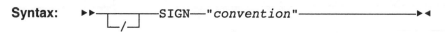

| **Parameters:** | *convention* | Either ASCII or EBCDIC. |

Properties:	Default:	SIGN"ASCII"
	Phase:	Syntax check
	Environment:	All
	$SET:	Initial

Dependencies: Set to SIGN"ASCII" immediately by CHARSET"ASCII".
Set to SIGN"EBCDIC" at end by CHARSET"EBCDIC".

TIME

Puts the time at the top of each page of the listing.

Syntax:

Parameters: None

Default: TIME

$SET: No

You can use this directive only with the DATE directive.

WARNING

Specifies the lowest severity level of errors to report.

Syntax:

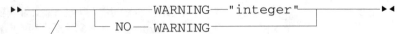

Parameters:

integer   1, 2, or 3.

Default: WARNING "1"

$SET: Any

The possible values of the parameter are:

1 only those of level U, S, or E.

2 only those of level U, S, E, or W.

3 all - that is, levels U, S, E, W, and I.

With NOWARNING only those of level U or S are reported.

XREF

Makes the compiler produce a cross-reference listing.

Syntax:

Parameters:	None
Default:	NOXREF
$SET:	No

The listing shows all data items and associated sequence numbers in alphabetical order. The sequence number shows the line where a data item is defined and is marked with a #. Further sequence numbers show where the item is used. The listing also shows what kind of data item it is, and its length in bytes if it is a group item. The listing continues with a similar description of the procedure names.

To produce the cross reference listing the compiler needs extra work space on the disk. The space needed depends on the number of data items and procedure-names and the number of times they are referenced.

Specifying XREF sets RESEQ.

This directive can be enabled by the Personal COBOL check menu **F7=ref** switch. Press the **F7** key until the word XREF appears on the information line.

Chapter 6

Run-Time System Error Messages

Overview

Personal COBOL includes a sophisticated run-time system which executes both user programs and Personal COBOL itself. If the run-time system encounters an error it will output an error message. This will generally occur while you are running or animating your program, but could also occur while compiling.

Most error messages produced while compiling (checking) will be for syntax errors detected by the compiler. Syntax errors are documented in the On-line Reference, not in this manual. Syntax errors are displayed as an error number and by a line of asterisks that ends where the compiler detected the error, followed by a line of text briefly outlining the cause.

This chapter lists the text and severity of each run-time error, explains the error or problem that causes the message, and gives advice on how to prevent it. Some errors are environment dependent, so will not be issued by the Personal COBOL System.

There are two types of run-time errors:

Fatal   A message is sent to the screen and the
                    program terminates immediately.

Recoverable   The error is reported to the program. You can
                    trap these errors in your program, but often

they are the result of an error in your program's logic. If the program does not trap the error a message is sent to the screen and the program terminates immediately.

List of Run-Time Errors

RT001   Insufficient buffer space

Severity: Recoverable

Explanation: You have tried to OPEN a file directly or indirectly and, although you have not ex-ceeded your system's file limit, something in your system is unable to allocate enough memory space for this operation.

Resolution: Although you can trap this error you must do STOP RUN as soon as it is reported.

RT002   File not open when access attempted

Severity: Recoverable

Explanation: You have tried to access a file without OPENing it first.

Resolution: OPEN the file with the open mode that you need and try the operation again. As this error implies there is an error in your program's logic you may want to terminate the run and correct your program.

RT003   Mode error

Severity: Recoverable

Explanation:	You are trying to execute a device not a program.
Resolution:	Open the device in the correct mode; or close any open files, do STOP RUN and correct your program.

RT004   Illegal file name

Severity:	Recoverable
Explanation:	A file-name contains an illegal character. This could be any character that is not part of the permitted character set or it could be the system-dependent delimiter, which on most systems is the space.
Resolution:	Try the file operation again using the correct file-name.

RT005   Illegal device specification

Severity:	Recoverable
Explanation:	Devices to which your COBOL program can write are defined by the operating system. You have tried to write to a device that is not defined by your system.
Resolution:	Try the operation again using a device name that your system recognizes.

RT006   Attempt to write to a file opened for INPUT

Severity:	Recoverable
Explanation:	You have tried to WRITE to a file that is open only for input.

Error Messages

Resolution: Close the file and open it with a mode such as I-O, which allows you to write to the file. As this error implies there is a mistake in your program's logic you may want to terminate the run and correct your program.

RT007   Disk space exhausted

Severity: Fatal

Explanation: The disk is full.

Resolution: This error can be trapped, but once it has been reported you must do a STOP RUN immediately to terminate your program's run. When your program has terminated, delete any files that you no longer need. Alternatively, if your operating system supports this, put a new disk in a floppy disk drive and redirect your program's file operations to this.

RT008   Attempt to input from a file opened for OUTPUT

Severity: Recoverable

Explanation: You have tried to read from a file that is open only for output.

Resolution: Close the file and open it with a mode such as I-O, which allows you to read from the file. As this error implies there is a mistake in your program's logic you may want to terminate the run and correct your program.

RT009   No room in directory

Severity: Recoverable

Explanation: The directory is full, or your program cannot find it.

Resolution: Delete any files that you no longer need. Alternatively, if your operating system supports this, put a new disk in a floppy disk drive and redirect your program's file operations to this. Alternatively, specify a different drive or directory for your file operations.

RT010   File name not supplied

Severity: Recoverable

Explanation: You have declared a file as an external file, but have not named it. This message occurs when you attempt to open that file.

Resolution: The only way you can continue at this point is if you are able to break out of your program, set up the external file name, then continue running your program. Otherwise, you should do STOP RUN, set up external file name, then run your program again.

RT012   Attempt to open a file which is already open

Severity: Recoverable

Explanation: You have tried to OPEN a file which is already OPEN and so cannot be OPENed again.

Resolution: Cancel your second attempt to OPEN the file. If the fact that the file is already OPEN is acceptable to you, continue to run your program.

RT013   File not found

Severity: Recoverable

Explanation: The operating system has been unable to find a file which you have attempted to access in your program.

Resolution: If your Operating System supports this, insert the correct diskette, that is the one which contains the required program, provided that no files are currently OPEN on the present diskette. If the error is the result of a spelling mistake then ask for the correct file and attempt the file operation again.

RT014   Too many files open simultaneously

Severity: Recoverable

Explanation: You have tried to exceed the maximum number of files which you can have OPEN at any one time. This may be a software or an operating-system restraint, but you must not violate it.

Resolution: CLOSE some of the OPEN files which you are not currently accessing, and then try to OPEN the relevant file again. You should then be able to continue to run your program. Depending on your Operating System, you may be able to increase the maximum number of files you are allowed to have OPEN.

RT015   Too many indexed files open

Severity: Recoverable

Explanation: You have tried to exceed the maximum number of ISAM files which you can have OPEN at any one time. This may be a software or an operating-system restraint, but you must not violate it.

Resolution: CLOSE some of the OPEN ISAM files which you are not currently accessing, and then try to OPEN the relevant file again. You should then be able to continue to run your program. Note that ISAM files count as two files, one for data and one for the index.

RT016   Too many device files open

Severity: Recoverable

Explanation: You have tried to exceed the maximum number of device files which you can have OPEN at any one time. This may be a software or an operating-system restraint, but you must not violate it.

Resolution: CLOSE some of the OPEN device files which you are not currently accessing, and then try to OPEN the relevant file again. You should then be able to continue to run your program.

RT017   Record error: probably zero length

Severity: Recoverable

Explanation: You have probably tried to access a record that has had no value moved into it.

Resolution: Although this error is recoverable in the sense that it can be trapped, once it has been reported you must execute a STOP RUN statement immediately and then recode your program to ensure that the COBOL record length is not zero.

RT018   Read part record error: eof before eor or file open in wrong mode

Severity: Recoverable

Explanation: A part record has been found at the end of a file. Consequently your Run-Time System will treat the data file as a record and not finding a full record will report this error.

Resolution: Ensure that the record size you give when you READ from or WRITE to a file is consistent.

RT019   Rewrite error: open mode or access mode wrong

Severity: Recoverable

Explanation: You are attempting to do a REWRITE to a file that has not been opened with the correct access mode for this operation.

Resolution: CLOSE the file and reOPEN it in a mode such as the I-O mode, which allows you to do REWRITE operations on that file. As this error implies that there is a mistake in the logic of your code you may like to recode your program having first CLOSEd any OPEN files, and then execute a STOP RUN statement.

RT020   Device or resource busy

Severity: Recoverable

Explanation: You have attempted to OPEN a file that is assigned to a device or resource (for example, a line printer) that is not available at this time.

Resolution: You can trap the error status returned by OPEN and retry the OPEN at regular intervals until it succeeds.

RT021   File is a directory

Severity: Fatal

Explanation: You have tried to WRITE to a directory instead of to a file.

Resolution: You will have to recode your program so that it WRITEs to a file and not to a directory.

RT022   Illegal or impossible access mode for OPEN

Severity: Recoverable

Explanation: The mode in which you are attempting to OPEN a file violates the general rule of COBOL programming for that type of file, for example you may have OPENed a line-sequential file in the I-O mode.

Resolution: OPEN the file with a mode that is compatible with that type of file.

RT023   Illegal or impossible access mode for CLOSE

Severity: Recoverable

Explanation: The mode in which you are attempting to CLOSE a file is not possible for that type of file.

Resolution: CLOSE the file with a new access mode which is compatible with that type of file, or execute

Error Messages

a STOP RUN statement and recode your
program.

RT024   Disk input-output error

Severity: Recoverable

Explanation: This error could be given if you do a READ
                   after a WRITE or if there is a verification
                   failure or a parity error.

Resolution: In some circumstances this error will be fatal,
                   but if it occurs during a READ you can trap it
                   and then do a CLOSE on the file before
                   executing a STOP RUN statement.

RT025   Operating system data error

Severity: Fatal

Explanation: You are trying to set up terminal characteris-
                   tics for a device which is not a terminal.

Resolution: Recode your program.

RT026   Block I-O error

Severity: Fatal

Explanation: An error has occurred while you are attempt
                   ing to access a disk. This could be the result
                   of a corrupt disk.

Resolution: If you have a corrupt disk try to run your
                   program again using your backup copy.

RT027   Device not available

Severity: Recoverable

Explanation: You are attempting to access a device which
                      is either not attached to your machine or if
                      attached is not online.

Resolution: Attach the device to your machine and ensure
                      that it is online. Repeat the file operation.

RT028   No space on device

Severity: Fatal

Explanation: You have attempted a file operation such as
                      WRITE for which there is not sufficient space
                      available on your disk.

Resolution: When your program has terminated you will
                      have to delete some of the files or directories
                      on your current logged in disk. Ensure that
                      you delete sufficient files on your disk so that
                      you have enough room to carry out successful
                      file operations.

RT029   Attempt to delete open file

Severity: Recoverable

Explanation: You have attempted to perform a DELETE FD
                      operation on an open file.

Resolution: Close the file before performing the DELETE
                      FD operation.

RT030   File system is read-only

Severity: Recoverable

Error Messages

Explanation: The file system which you are using is READ only, which effectively means that it is WRITE protected. You have tried to amend the information found within a file in some way, for example you may have tried to WRITE to a file or to DELETE information found within it. As the file system which you are using is READ only you can only READ the contents of its files, you cannot alter them in any way.

Resolution: You will have to abandon your attempt to alter the information within the file unless you can take your own personal copy of that file. You should then be able to alter the contents of your copy, but not of the original source.

RT031   Not owner of file

Severity: Recoverable

Explanation: You are attempting an operation on a file but the file's owner has not given you the necessary permission for that operation. You could for example be attempting to alter the access modes for a file, which only the file's owner can do.

Resolution: You will have to abandon your attempted file operation unless the file's owner gives you the permission necessary to do the operation you wish to carry out.

RT032   Too many indexed files, or no such process

Severity: Recoverable

Explanation: You have tried to OPEN an indexed file but the number of files that you currently have open is the system limit.

Resolution: You will have to CLOSE some of the indexed files which you are no longer accessing, and you should then be able to OPEN the file you require.

RT033   Physical I-O error

Severity: Fatal

Explanation: You have a hardware error of some type, perhaps you have failed to place a disk in the relevant drive or you may have tried to WRITE to a disk but the processor detected hardware interface has failed.

Resolution: You will have to try to correct the fault in your hardware, for example by placing a disk in the necessary drive.

RT034   Incorrect mode or file descriptor

Severity: Recoverable

Explanation: You are either trying to WRITE to a file which is open for READ purposes only, or READ a file which is open for WRITE purposes only.

Resolution: You will need to CLOSE the file and reopen using the correct access mode. As this error implies that there is a mistake in the logic of your program you may want to CLOSE any OPEN files, execute a STOP RUN statement and then recode your program to eliminate the logic error.Note:Sharable files opened INPUT (READ only) by the COBOL system will still require WRITE permission (from the operating system) to enable temporary locking to take place.

RT035 Attempt to access a file with incorrect permission

Severity: Recoverable

Explanation: You are attempting a file operation which you do not have sufficient permission to achieve. For example you could be trying to WRITE data to a file which has been set up with the READ attribute only.

Resolution: If you are the owner of the file you will be able to alter the attributes of the file so that you have the permission needed to effect the particular file operation you were attempting. If you are not the owner of the file you will not be able to carry out that operation successfully unless you copy the file and make the changes to the copy only. You will not be able to alter the source file.

RT036 File already exists

Severity: Recoverable

Explanation: You are attempting an inappropriate operation on an already existing file.

Resolution: As this error implies a fault in your program's logic you may like to recode your program to eliminate this mistake.

RT037 File access denied

Severity: Fatal

Explanation: Your attempt to access a file has been denied by the operating system. You may have tried to WRITE to a write-protected file or you could have attempted to READ from an OUTPUT device.

Resolution: Alter the access permission on the relevant file. Access can be READ only, if you just want to read the contents of the file without making any changes, or it can be READ and WRITE in which case you will be able to alter its contents.

RT038   Disk not compatible

Severity: Fatal

Explanation: You have tried to load a disk that is incompatible with the current version of your operating system. This could be because it was created under a previous version of the system or it could have been created under a completely different operating system. You would also receive this error if you tried to load a disk with a name that clashed with a disk that was already loaded.

Resolution: If the error is a result of a clash of names you can rename one of the disks and then you will be able to load both disks together if this is what you require.

RT039   File not compatible

Severity: Fatal

Explanation: You are trying to load a file that is not compatible with the structure of files under the current release of your software. This could be because the file was created either under a different operating system or under a previous version of your current system.

Resolution: You will need to create a new copy of the file which has the correct structure.

Error Messages

RT040   National Language Variants not set up correctly

Severity:	Fatal
Explanation:	You have attempted to use the additional language variants at run-time, but the environment or side file that is required to set up the language either has not been set up correctly, or does not exist, or is invalid.
Resolution:	Set up the required environment or side file before you attempt to run the program again.

RT041   Corrupt indexed file

Severity:	Recoverable
Explanation:	Your Run-Time System does not recognize the control information for an indexed file and as the index has been corrupted in some way the data within the file is no longer accessible by your system. This error is recoverable in the sense that it can be trapped but should you receive it there is little you can do except to CLOSE any OPEN files and stop your program's run.
Resolution:	You will have to rerun your program using the backup copy of that file.

RT042   Attempt to write on broken pipe

Severity:	Recoverable
Explanation:	Your program has created a process as a result of a DD_logical filename mapping assignment (for example, the process may be a line printer spooler). The process was not created properly, or has died prematurely. This error occurs when your program attempts to write to the process.

Resolution: You can trap the error status returned by the write operation, then open the file again.

RT043   File information missing for indexed file

Severity: Fatal

Explanation: You normally receive this error if the system crashed on the program's previous run, while the file was OPEN. Information was probably added to the end of the file, but the directory information was not updated and so that data cannot be accessed by your system. You can also receive this error if you copied the indexed file from one disk to another but only copied either the data part of the file or the index.

Resolution: If the error is the result of a crash then whether you can access the necessary data or not is entirely system dependent. If however it is the result of a faulty copy you should be able to restore the missing part of the file from the .dat or .idx file.

RT047   Indexed structure overflow

Severity: Fatal

Explanation: There is some fault in the structure of your indexed file. You have probably tried to put another entry in the index when there is no room for it. This error could also be given if you have tried to access an old format indexed file, created perhaps using CIS COBOL.

Resolution: If there is no room in your index for further entries you will have to reorganize your file.

RT065   File locked

Severity: Recoverable

Explanation: You have tried to OPEN a file which has
                     already been locked, or opened for output by
                     another user. Alternatively, you have tried to
                     lock or OPEN for output a file which another
                     user already has open.

Resolution: Your program can inform the system operator
                     (if there is one) that it is unable to access this
                     file and should wait until the other user has
                     finished using the file and closes it. You
                     should then be able to continue to run your
                     program.

RT066   Attempt to add duplicate record key to indexed file

Severity: Fatal

Explanation: You have tried to add a duplicate key for a
                     key which you have not defined as being able
                     to have duplicates.

Resolution: As this error implies that there is a fault in the
                     logic of your program you will probably
                     need to recode.

RT067   Indexed file not open

Severity: Recoverable

Explanation: You are attempting to access an indexed file
                     which you have not OPENed.

Resolution: OPEN the file in the relevant access mode and
                     then retry the unsuccessful file operation.

RT068   Record locked

Severity: Recoverable

Explanation: You have tried to access a record which is
                     currently locked by another user.

Resolution: Your program should inform the systems
                     operator (if one exists) that the record is
                     currently locked, and you should then wait
                     until the other user has released the lock on
                     that record. You should then be able to access
                     the relevant record. You should not
                     continually retry to gain access to the record
                     without operator intervention, as this could
                     result in your application hanging.

RT069   Illegal argument to ISAM module

Severity: Fatal

Explanation: This is the result of an internal system error.

Resolution: Contact Technical Support who will try to
                     help you discover the cause of your error and
                     how it can be rectified.

RT070   Too many indexed files open

Severity: Recoverable

Explanation: You are attempting to OPEN an indexed file
                     but you have already exhausted the system
                     limit which specifies how many of these files
                     can be OPENed at any one time.

Resolution: CLOSE some of the open indexed files which
                     you are not currently accessing. You should
                     then be able to OPEN the indexed file which
                     you require and to continue the program run.

Error Messages

RT071　Bad indexed file format

Severity:　　　　Fatal

Explanation:　　This error could be given if you are using a
file which has been corrupted, otherwise it is
the result of an internal system error.

Resolution:　　If the disk you are using is corrupt rerun your
program using your backup copy of the disk.
If this is not the cause of the error then you
should contact Technical Support who will
try to discover the cause of your error and
how it can be rectified.

RT072　End of indexed file

Severity:　　　　Fatal

Explanation:　　This is the result of an internal system error.

Resolution:　　Contact Technical Support who will try to
help you discover the cause of your error and
how it can be rectified.

RT073　No record found in indexed file

Severity:　　　　Fatal

Explanation:　　This is the result of an internal system error.

Resolution:　　Contact Technical Support who will try to
help you discover the cause of the error and
how it may be rectified.

RT074   No current record in indexed file

Severity: Fatal

Explanation: This is the result of an internal system error.

Resolution: Contact Technical Support who will try to
help you discover the cause of the error and
how it may be rectified.

RT075   Indexed data file name too long

Severity: Fatal

Explanation: The maximum number of characters that the
UNIX system allows a file name to have, is 14.
However when using ISAM, the extension
.IDX is added to the end of the user-defined
file name, and so your file name must not
exceed 10 characters in length, otherwise you
will receive this error.

Resolution: Rename the file with a shorter file name, that
is, one that is less than 10 characters in length.

RT076   Can't create lock file in /ISAM directory

Severity: Fatal

Explanation: For some reason your system is unable to
create a lock file in the ISAM directory. One
reason for this could be that in its previous
run your program terminated abnormally
(perhaps due to a power failure) leaving some
files locked. When you try to run this
program following its abnormal termination
you will receive this error.

Resolution: You will have to manually remove all of the
files that are still locked from the ISAM
directory before you can successfully run
your program.

Error Messages

RT077   Internal ISAM module error

Severity: Fatal

Explanation: This is the result of an internal system error.

Resolution: Contact Technical Support who will try to help you discover the cause of your error and how it can be rectified.

RT078   Illegal key description in indexed file

Severity: Fatal

Explanation: This is the result of an internal system error.

Resolution: Contact Technical Support who will try to help you discover the cause of your error and how it can be rectified.

RT081   Key already exists in indexed file

Severity: Fatal

Explanation: This is the result of an internal system error.

Resolution: Contact Technical Support who will try to help you discover the cause of your error and how it can be rectified.

RT100   Invalid file operation

Severity: Fatal

Explanation: You have attempted a file operation which violates a general rule of COBOL in some way. The most likely cause of this error is that you have attempted a REWRITE on a sequential file opened I-O, or on a relative file with access mode sequential also opened I-O, without preceding it with a successful READ NEXT.

Resolution: Recode your program to ensure that the offending REWRITE statement is preceded by a READ NEXT.

RT101   Illegal operation on an indexed file

Severity: Fatal

Explanation: This is the result of an internal system error.

Resolution: Contact Technical Support who will try to help you discover the cause of your error and how it can be rectified.

RT102   Sequential file with non-integral number of records

Severity: Fatal

Explanation: This error could be given if:

- you have specified an incorrect record length for a sequential file

- the sequential file you are attempting to access is corrupt in some way

- the file which you have specified is not a sequential file.

Resolution: Recode your program so that it specifies the correct type of file, or if the error is the result of a corrupt file, attempt to run the program again using a backup copy of that file.

RT104   Null file name used in file operation

Severity: Fatal

Explanation: You have specified a variable name for a
                    filename instead of a literal, so on attempting
                    to OPEN that file only spaces are found.

Resolution: Recode your program specifying the correct
                    filename.

RT105   Memory allocation error

Severity: Fatal

Explanation: The Run-Time System is unable to allocate
                    sufficient memory space to successfully carry
                    out the attempted operation. This error
                    implies that there is no memory space left on
                    your system.

Resolution: You will have to obtain more memory in
                    which to run your program. Refer to your
                    Operating System documentation for details
                    of how you can obtain more memory, if this is
                    possible.

RT106   Dictionary error

Severity: Fatal

Explanation: This could be the result of a READ or WRITE
                    error to file or disk, but it is more likely to be
                    the result of an internal system error.

Resolution: Contact Technical Support who will try to
                    help you to discover the cause of your error
                    and how it may be rectified.

RT107   Operation not implemented on this Run-Time System

Severity: Fatal

Explanation: You are attempting to do a file operation which your Run-Time System does not support.

Resolution: You will have to recode your program so that it does not attempt such operations, or you will have to acquire a version of your system that does support this facility.

RT108   Failure to initialize data division

Severity: Fatal

Explanation: The Run-Time System cannot load your program properly because the data needed to correctly initialize the Data Divison has become corrupted.

Resolution: You should compile your program again to try to obtain good intermediate code.

RT109   Invalid checksum in Run-Time System

Severity: Recoverable

Explanation: The internal information within the Run-Time System has been altered. This error may be caused by a corrupted Run-Time System, or you may have illegally attempted to change the internal Run-Time System information.

Resolution: Contact Technical Support who will try to help you to discover the cause of the error and how it may be rectified.

RT116   Cannot allocate memory

Severity: Fatal

Explanation: For some reason a part of your Run-Time
                    System is unable to allocate you sufficient
                    memory to enable you to execute your code.

Resolution: You should try to reduce memory usage by
                    cancelling programs that are not in use, then
                    attempt the operation that caused this
                    message again.

RT117   Bad collating sequence

Severity: Fatal

Explanation: This is an internal system error.

Resolution: Please contact Technical Support who will try
                    to help you to discover the cause of the error
                    and how it may be rectified.

RT118   Symbol not found

Severity: Fatal

Explanation: You are unable to load your object file. You
                    could receive this error if you attempt to call a
                    program that has not been specified in the
                    COBPATH environment variable.

Resolution: Check to see that your COBPATH has been
                    set up correctly. If not, amend your
                    COBPATH to include the program being
                    called.

RT119   Symbol redefined

Severity: Fatal

Explanation: You are unable to load your object file because it has an entry point with the same name as a module already loaded.

Resolution: Once your program has terminated recode it to remove the naming duplication. Resubmit your program to your COBOL system.

RT120   Symbol string table of zero size

Severity: Fatal

Explanation: You probably have a malformed object file.

Resolution: Once the program has terminated you will need to correct your object file. If this does not work, contact Technical Support who will try to help you to discover the specific cause of the error.

RT121   Symbol is not in text section

Severity: Fatal

Explanation: You have attempted to CALL a subprogram that is not an executable program.

Resolution: Check that the subprogram being CALLed is an executable one. If required, correct the subprogram's name in the CALLing program and resubmit it to your COBOL system. Alternatively, you have used the same name for a called program as a previously defined data-item. Once your program has terminated, recode it to remove the naming duplication. Resubmit your program to your COBOL system.

Error Messages

6-27

RT122   Coblongjmp called below level of cobsetjmp

Severity: Fatal

Explanation: You may have returned control to a higher level in the CALL/PERFORM hierarchy than the level at which cobsetjmp was called. Coblongjmp must only be called from the same or from a lower level in the CALL/PERFORM hierarchy as cobsetjmp was. See your Operating Guide for details of cobsetjmp and coblongjmp.

Resolution: Check and correct the logic of your program, and then resubmit your program to your COBOL system.

RT123   Unknown relocation type

Severity: Fatal

Explanation: You are using incompatible versions of the object file and the COBOL run-time library.

Resolution: Once the program has terminated, you will need to resubmit your object file to your COBOL system with the current version of your COBOL run-time library. If this does not work, contact Technical Support who will try to help you to discover the specific cause of the error.

RT129   Attempt to access record zero of relative file

Severity: Recoverable

Explanation: The value specified in the RELATIVE KEY data-item contains the value zero.

Resolution: You should ensure that the value in the
RELATIVE KEY data-item is greater than
zero, then continue to run your program.

RT135   File not found

Severity: Recoverable

Explanation: The operating system has been unable to find
a file which you have attempted to access in
your program.

Resolution: If your operating system supports this, insert
the correct diskette (that is the one which
contains the required program) provided that
no files are currently OPEN on the present
diskette. If the error is the result of a spelling
mistake then ask for the correct file and
attempt the file operation again.

RT137   Open mode not supported for this file

Severity: Recoverable

Explanation: You are trying to open a device in an illegal
mode; for example, opening a printer for
input.

Resolution: Either the assignment of a file name is
incorrrect, or your program needs to be
changed.

RT138   File closed with lock - cannot be opened

Severity: Recoverable

Explanation: You are attempting to OPEN a file which you
previously CLOSEd with lock, and because
such an operation violates one of the general

rules of COBOL programming you have been given this error.

Resolution: You will not be able to OPEN the relevant file. As this error implies that you have made a mistake in the logical structure of your program, you will probably want to CLOSE any remaining OPEN files, execute a STOP RUN statement and recode.

RT139   Record length or key data inconsistency

Severity: Recoverable

Explanation: There is a discrepancy between the length of a record, or the keys which you have specified, in your current program and its definition in the program in which it was first OPENed.

Resolution: This error implies that there is a fault in your program so you will probably need to edit your code, then resubmit it to your COBOL system before running it again.

RT141   File already open - cannot be opened

Severity: Recoverable

Explanation: You have tried to OPEN a file which is already OPEN and so cannot be OPENed again.

Resolution: Cancel your second attempt to OPEN the file and continue to run your program if the fact that the file is already OPEN is acceptable to you. However as this error implies that there is an error in the logic of your program you may wish to CLOSE any OPEN files, execute a STOP RUN statement and then edit your program to correct the fault in its logic.

RT142   File not open - cannot be closed

Severity: Recoverable

Explanation: You have tried to CLOSE a file which is not
                     OPEN which is impossible to achieve.

Resolution: You can abandon your attempt to CLOSE the
                     relevant file and continue to run your
                     program. However as this error implies that
                     there is a mistake in the logic of your program
                     you may wish to CLOSE any OPEN files,
                     execute a STOP RUN statement and then edit
                     your program to correct the fault in its logic.

RT143   Rewrite/delete in sequential mode not preceded by successful read

Severity: Recoverable

Explanation: You have violated one of the general rules of
                     COBOL programming as you have failed to
                     do a successful READ on a sequentially
                     accessed file prior to attempting a REWRITE
                     or DELETE on some of the information
                     contained within that file.

Resolution: If the previous READ was successful then
                     perform a READ on the relevant file before
                     you retry the unsuccessful REWRITE or
                     DELETE operation. If the previous READ
                     was also unsuccessful CLOSE the file execute
                     a STOP RUN statement and then recode your
                     program before you next run it.

RT144   Boundary Violation

Severity: Recoverable

Explanation: You have attempted to WRITE or REWRITE a
                     record which is larger than the largest, or

Error Messages

smaller than the smallest record allowed by the RECORD IS VARYING clause of the associated file.

Resolution:

You should change the length of the record you wish to write so that it fits within the boundaries defined in the record description entry of the associated file.

RT146 No current record defined for sequential read

Severity:

Recoverable

Explanation:

The file position indicator in your file is undefined owing to a failed READ/START or INVALID KEY condition. You have tried to read another record in the file but as the current record is undefined the system cannot find the start of the record for which you have asked.

Resolution:

You should attempt a START op and continue to do so until the file position indicator is updated successfully.

RT147 Wrong open mode or access mode for read/start

Severity:

Recoverable

Explanation:

You have violated one of the general rules of COBOL programming as you have tried to carry out a READ or START opration on a file which has not been OPENed for INPUT or I-O, or is not OPEN at all.

Resolution:

OPEN the file for I-O or for INPUT and you should then be able to continue to run your program. However, as this error implies that there is a mistake in the logic of your program

you may want to CLOSE any files which are
OPEN, execute a STOP RUN statement and
then edit you code in order to rectify the fault
in its logic.

RT148   Wrong open mode or access mode for write

Severity: Recoverable

Explanation: You have tried to WRITE to a file in
                     sequential access mode that you have not
                     OPENed for OUTPUT or EXTEND, or you
                     have tried to WRITE to a file in random or
                     dynamic access mode that has not been
                     OPENed INPUT or I-O.

Resolution: CLOSE the file and re-OPEN it with the
                     correct open mode for the file type. However,
                     as this error implies that there is an error in
                     the logic of your program you may want to
                     CLOSE any files that are OPEN, execute a
                     STOP RUN statement and then edit your code
                     to rectify the fault in its logic.

RT149   Wrong open mode or access mode for rewrite/delete

Severity: Recoverable

Explanation: You have violated one of the general rules of
                     COBOL syntax as you are trying to do a
                     REWRITE or a DELETE on a file that you
                     have not OPENed for I-O.

Resolution: CLOSE the file and reOPEN for I-O.
                     However, as the implication of this error is
                     that your program contains a logic error you
                     may wish to CLOSE any OPEN files, execute
                     a STOP RUN statement and then edit your
                     code to eliminate the error in its logic.

Error Messages

RT150　Program abandoned at user request

Severity:　　Fatal

Explanation:　You have interrupted the program by means of a keyboard interrupt. The program is closed down, and any open files closed automatically by the Run-Time System.

RT151　Random read on sequential file

Severity:　　Recoverable

Explanation:　You have violated one of the general rules of COBOL syntax as you are trying to do a random READ on a file which has sequential organization.

Resolution:　READ the file with the correct access mode. As this error implies that there is an error in your program's logic you may like to CLOSE any files which are OPEN, execute a STOP RUN statement and recode your program to eliminate the mistakes in its logic.

RT152　REWRITE on file not open I-O

Severity:　　Recoverable

Explanation:　You have violated one of the general rules of COBOL syntax as you have attempted a REWRITE on a file that is not OPEN I-O.

Resolution:　CLOSE the relevant file and re-OPEN it for I-O operations. You should then be able to carry out the REWRITE operation successfully. However, as this error implies that there is a logic fault in the coding of your program you may wish to CLOSE any OPEN files, execute a STOP RUN statement and then edit your code to eliminate the logic mistake.

RT153   Subscript out of range

Severity: Fatal

Explanation: A subscript which you have used in your program is out of the defined range, that is, it is either less than one or it is greater than the number of occurrences of the item.

Resolution: You will need to recode your program.

RT154   PERFORM nested too deeply

Severity: Fatal

Explanation: This error usually results if you have used GO TO to jump out of the range of a PERFORM rather than to jump to an EXIT statement at the end of its range.

Resolution: When your program has terminated you will need to recode your program to ensure that the GO TO in question jumps to an EXIT statement at the end of the PERFORM's range. You should then be able to successfully run your program.

RT155   Illegal command line

Severity: Fatal

Explanation: The generic command line interpreter, which must be present if your program is to be run successfully, is not found on your system.

Resolution: Make sure that the interpreter is present to enable your system to pick up the commands correctly and then rerun your program.

Error Messages

RT156   Too many parentheses in a compute statement

Severity: Fatal

Explanation: You have coded a compute statement which is too complex for your system to handle successfully.

Resolution: You will have to recode your program. We strongly advise you to break the relevant compute statement into a number of simpler statements.

RT157   Not enough program memory: object file too large to load

Severity: Recoverable

Explanation: Either your program is too large for the available memory space, or the stack is full.

Resolution: If you have specified the ON OVERFLOW/ EXCEPTION clause in the relevant CALL statement the error is recoverable. Any associated imperative statement will be executed before the next instruction.

RT158   Attempt to REWRITE to a line-sequential file

Severity: Recoverable

Explanation: You have used the REWRITE statement in conjunction with a file whose organization is line sequential. The REWRITE statement cannot be used with line sequential files.

Resolution: Close the offending file before executing a STOP RUN statement to ensure that you do not lose any data from it. Recode your program to make the organization of the file to which you wish to do a REWRITE either sequential, indexed sequential, or relative.

RT159   Malformed line-sequential file

Severity: Recoverable

Explanation: A line-sequential file which you are trying to access is corrupt in some way.

Resolution: Rerun your program using the backup copy of that file.

RT160   Overlay loading error

Severity: Recoverable

Explanation: An error has occurred while trying to load the intermediate code for an independent segment. The segment is either missing or corrupted in some way.

Resolution: If the segment is missing, locate it. If you cannot find it, or if it is present and corrupt, resubmit your program to your COBOL system.

RT161   Illegal intermediate code

Severity: Fatal

Explanation: The intermediate code which is currently being processed is not valid code. You are probably trying to execute a corrupted file or one which has not been submitted to your COBOL system successfully.

Resolution: You will have to resubmit your source program to your COBOL system, to try to obtain uncorrupted intermediate code.

RT162   Arithmetic overflow or underflow

Severity: Fatal

Explanation: You have attempted to divide a data-item by zero.

Resolution: You will need to recode your program to avoid this illegal operation.

RT163   Illegal character in numeric field

Severity: Fatal

Explanation: By default the value which you enter into a numeric or numeric-edited field is checked to ensure that it is numeric. If any of the characters are found to be non- numeric then you will receive this error. The error can also be given if you have entered uninitialized numerics into numeric or numeric-edited fields, as these are automatically space filled and are thus classified as non-numeric items.

Resolution: If you unset the numeric field check switch on the run command line then the Run-Time System will not check that all values in a numeric or numeric-edited field are numeric and you should be able to run your program successfully. Alternatively, you can make sure that you initialize numeric and numeric-edited items with numeric values, which should enable your program to run successfully regardless of the setting of the numeric field check switch.

RT164 Run-time subprogram not found

Severity: Fatal

Explanation: You have attempted to call a subroutine whose entry address has not been set up in your Run-Time System.

Resolution: Check to see that you used a valid call number in the unsuccessful subroutine call. If not, amend your code to contain a call number which your system recognizes. If you did use a valid call number but still received this error you should contact Technical Support.

RT165 Version number incompatibility

Severity: Fatal

Explanation: You are using intermediate code which has been produced on a version of your COBOL system that is incompatible with the Run-Time System you are currently using. Your RTS, herefore, will not be able to execute correctly any generated code you are producing or have already produced from this intermediate code. Alternatively, you may have attempted to execute a file which is not your COBOL system's intermediate or generated code.

Resolution: Resubmit your source programs to your COBOL system using the new version of your software.

Error Messages

RT166   Recursive COBOL CALL is illegal

Severity: Fatal

Explanation: You have tried to CALL a COBOL module
                   that is already active.

Resolution: You will need to recode your program.

RT167   Too many USING items

Severity: Fatal

Explanation: The list of items which you have supplied in a
                   CALL....USING statement is longer than the
                   Run-Time System can handle.

Resolution: Once your program has terminated recode it
                   with group items rather than elementary
                   items before rerunning it.

RT168   Stack overflow

Severity: Fatal

Explanation: You have nested a PERFORM statement or a
                   series of CALL statements too deeply.

Resolution: Edit your program to reduce the number of
                   levels within a nested PERFORM or CALL
                   statement, then resubmit your source code to
                   your COBOL system.

RT169   Illegal configuration information

Severity: Fatal

Explanation: You have attempted an operation for which
                   your machine is not configured; the most
                   likely cause of this is that ADIS is not
                   configured correctly.

Resolution: Check that ADIS is configured correctly. See your Operating Guide for details of how you can reconfigure ADIS.

RT170   System program not found

Severity: Fatal

Explanation: A system program, for example ADIS or EXTFH, is not present on the current logged-in drive.

Resolution: Ensure that all the system programs are available on the logged-in drive and copy those which are not currently present using your backup system disk. Once all the necessary system programs are available you will be able to run your program.

RT171   Japanese operations illegal with this RTS

Severity: Fatal

Explanation: You are attempting to do Japanese operations with a non-Japanese Run-Time System, or you have used a Japanese version of your COBOL system to produce code which you are now trying to run using a non-Japanese Run-Time System.

Resolution: You will have to resubmit your program using a non-Japanese Run-Time System, or if you still want your program to perform Japanese operations then you will have to acquire a Japanese Run-Time system.

RT172   Recursive non-MF PERFORM is illegal

Severity: Fatal

Explanation: You have tried full recursion of a PERFORM
                      statement in a program that was submitted to
                      your COBOL system with the OSVS
                      parameter of the PERFORM-TYPE directive
                      specified. That is, you have attempted to end
                      two PERFORMs with the same return
                      address.

Resolution: You should either resubmit your program to
                      your COBOL system with a parameter other
                      than OSVS specified for the PERFORM-TYPE
                      directive, or recode your program so that each
                      PERFORM has its own unique return address
                      before you resubmit it to your COBOL system
                      with the MF parameter of the PERFORM-
                      TYPE directive specified.

RT173   Called program file not found in drive/
            directory

Severity: Fatal

Explanation: You have attempted to call a file which is not
                      present on your current logged-in drive or
                      directory, or in a directory pointed to by the
                      COBDIR environment variable.

Resolution: Once your program has terminated you will
                      need to copy the relevant file into your
                      logged-in drive or directory. If there is not
                      sufficient space available to allow you to do
                      this, then you will have to set the COBDIR
                      environment variable to search the directory
                      or drive on which the file is present when
                      your program calls it. Refer to your
                      Operating Guide for details of the COBDIR
                      environment variable. Once you have taken
                      these steps, run your program again.

RT175   Attempt to run intermediate code program which had severe errors in it

Severity:	Fatal
Explanation:	You are attempting to run a program that produced severe faults when you submitted it to your COBOL system with the run-time switch E turned off.
Resolution:	You should edit your source code to correct all the severe faults, resubmit to your COBOL system, then run the intermediate code that is produced. Note that when your program is being animated, ANIMATOR will report this error and will allow you to continue to run the program.

RT176   Illegal inter segment reference

Severity:	Fatal
Explanation:	You may have a corrupted file. Alternatively, your code contains a segment reference for the Forward Reference Table which is illegal.
Resolution:	Resubmit your source code to your COBOL system. If you receive this error again, contact Technical Support who will try to help you to discover the specific cause of the error.

RT177   Attempt to cancel active program

Severity:	Fatal
Explanation:	You have tried to remove a currently executing program or its parents or grandparents, from memory.

Error Messages

Resolution: Once your program has terminated you will
               need to recode your program to ensure that
               you do not attempt to cancel a program (or its
               parents or grandparents) while it is still being
               executed.

RT178   Error during save

Severity: Fatal

Explanation: You cannot save the information which your
               program has generated. This can be caused by
               several different reasons but one of the most
               common causes is that you have attempted to
               BUILD a module that is too large for the
               available memory space.

Resolution: If the error is caused by a lack of space you
               can either delete some of the files which you
               no longer need on your current disk, or insert
               a new floppy disk to take the output from
               your program. You should then be able to
               rerun your program and save the information
               given by it.

RT179   Error during chain

Severity: Program not found

Explanation: You have tried to chain to another program
               which your system is unable to find.

Resolution: Once your program has terminated you will
               need to copy the relevant file into your
               logged-in drive or directory. If there is not
               sufficient space available to allow you to do
               this, then you will have to set the COBDIR
               environment variable to search the directory
               or drive on which the file is present when
               your program calls it. Refer to your
               Operating Guide for details of the COBDIR

environment variable. Once you have taken these steps, run your program again.

RT180   End-of-file marker error

Severity: Fatal

Explanation: A file-marker used to indicate that the end-of-file has been reached is missing from one of your files.

Resolution: You will need to resubmit your code to your COBOL system, or use a debugger to place the end-of-file marker at the end of the file. You can then rerun your program.

RT181   Invalid parameter error

Severity: Fatal

Explanation: A parameter which you have used is not one which is recognized by your system. You have probably used a parameter for a Run-Time System subprogram which is not within the first 64K of the Data Division.

Resolution: Amend your code to contain a parameter which is known by your system. That is, ensure that the parameter is within the first 64K of the Data Division.

RT182   Console Input or Console Output open in wrong direction

Severity: Fatal

Explanation: You are either trying to READ input from the screen or WRITE to the keyboard.

Resolution: You will have to recode your program.

Error Messages

RT183   Attempt to open line-sequential file for I-O

Severity: Fatal

Explanation: You have tried to open a line-sequential file in the input-output open mode, but this mode is not supported for files with this organization.

Resolution: When your program has terminated you will have to recode your program to ensure that the file with organization line sequential is opened for input, output, or extend. You will then be able to rerun your code.

RT184   ACCEPT/DISPLAY I-O error

Severity: Fatal

Explanation: You have either tried to READ input from the screen or WRITE to the keyboard, or the ADIS module has not been able to open your terminal's channels for I-O.

Resolution: Your program contains an error in its logic so you will need to recode.

RT187   Run-Time System not found on $COBDIR path

Severity: Fatal

Explanation: The Run-Time System cannot be found on the path you have set up in the COBDIR environment variable. Alternatively, you may not have installed your COBOL system correctly.

Resolution: Ensure that the Run-Time System is on the path you have set up in the COBDIR environment variable. Alternatively, ensure that your COBOL system has been installed correctly. If it has not, you must reinstall your COBOL system, using the information given on installing your software in your Release Notes.

RT188   File name too large

Severity: Fatal

Explanation: A file name which you have used has more characters than the maximum number allowed by your operating system.

Resolution: Once your program has terminated you will need to recode your program, renaming the offending file with a shorter file name. You will then be able to run your program again.

RT189   Intermediate code load error

Severity: Fatal

Explanation: You are unable to load your intermediate code. You could receive this error if you attempt to load intermediate code that either has not been successfully produced, or has been corrupted in some way.

Resolution: Try to obtain good intermediate code, for example, by resubmitting (or submitting) your source code to your COBOL system. You should then be able to load your code and run the program successfully.

Error Messages

RT190   Too many arguments to CALL

Severity: Fatal

Explanation: A CALL within your program cannot be
                      successfully executed because of the number
                      of arguments which you have used with it.

Resolution: When your program has terminated you can
                      recode it using group items rather than
                      elementary ones. You should then be able to
                      run your program successfully.

RT191   Terminal type not defined

Severity: Fatal

Explanation: Your terminal is not defined in: the termcap
                      file in COBDIR, or the terminfo database, or
                      the cobcap file(depending on your
                      environment). Your operating system is
                      therefore unable to drive your terminal as it
                      has no environment specification for it.

Resolution: Set up the necessary environment for your
                      terminal.

RT192   Required terminal capability description missing

Severity: Fatal

Explanation: A compulsory entry, for example cursor
                      movement or clear screen, is missing from
                      your terminal configuration database
                      ("termdesc" or "termcap").

Resolution: Add the missing entry to your terminal
                      configuration database ("termdesc" or
                      "termcap").

RT193   Error in variable length count

Severity: Fatal

Explanation: The intermediate code which is currently
                     being processed is not a valid operation. You
                     are probably trying to execute a corrupt file or
                     one which has not been produced.

Resolution: You will have to resubmit your source code to
                     your COBOL system.

RT194   File size too large

Severity: Fatal

Explanation: A file which your program is accessing is too
                     large for successful execution to continue.

Resolution: When your program has terminated you
                     should recode your program spreading the
                     data over more than one file to ensure that no
                     file becomes too large for your operating
                     system to handle. Having recoded your
                     program you can then rerun it.

RT195   DELETE/REWRITE not preceded by a
            read

Severity: Fatal

Explanation: Before a DELETE or a REWRITE statement
                     can be successfully executed in sequential
                     access mode the last input-output statement
                     executed for the associated file must have
                     been a successful READ. In your code no
                     READ statement precedes your attempted
                     DELETE or REWRITE.

Error Messages

Resolution: When your program has terminated recode
                 your program making sure that the last input-
                 output statement to be executed before the
                 DELETE or REWRITE is a READ statement.

RT196   Record number too large in relative or indexed file

Severity: Fatal

Explanation: The relative record key has exceeded the
                 system limit, that is, the file is too large for the
                 system to handle.

Resolution: Alternatively, the record key which you have
                 specified is too large for the system to deal
                 with successfully, or the pointer to the record
                 has been corrupted in some way so that it is
                 either too large or it is not a multiple of the
                 record length.

RT197   Screen handling system initialization error

Severity: Fatal

Explanation: This error may be caused by one of the
                 following:

                 •   your display adapter is in the wrong
                      mode

                 •   your screen handling interface has not
                      been correctly initialized because
                      your terminal does not have the
                      required capabilities

                 •   memory has been incorrectly
                      allocated.

Resolution: If you are using a DOS or OS/2 system, the monitor must be in alphanumeric display mode rather than graphics display mode. You can set the display mode to a valid alphanumeric mode by using the DOS MODE utility and then rerunning your program. If your memory has been incorrectly allocated, you must rerun your program.

RT198   Load failure

Severity: Fatal

Explanation: The system cannot load a program, usually because there is insufficient memory.

Resolution: Rerun your program having made more memory available.

RT199   Operating system error out of defined range

Severity: Fatal

Explanation: A system call has returned an unexpected error number which is not documented.

Resolution: Contact Technical Support who will try to help you to discover the specific cause of this error.

RT200   Run-Time system internal logic error

Severity: Fatal

Explanation: You can receive this error if the amount of memory available on your machine is so low that not even the Run-Time System can be fully loaded properly. In this case you will

Error Messages

have to free some memory and then you should be able to run your program successfully.

Resolution: However, the most common cause of this error is that your Run-Time System has halted as a result of an internal logic error from which you cannot recover. If this is the case, you will need to contact Technical Support who will try to help you to discover the cause of the error.

RT201   I-O error in paging system

Severity: Fatal

Explanation: There is no room available in your current directory or on the floppy disk which you are using, for the paging file.

Resolution: When your program has terminated, delete some files which you no longer need in your directory to make room for the paging file or insert a new floppy disk.

RT202   Exported functionality error

Severity: Fatal

Explanation: You have either caused an internal Run-Time System error by invalid use of an exported function, or the code produced by a preprocessor within your COBOL system contains errors.

Resolution: Ensure that all of your external assembler applications call and use Run-Time System functions correctly before you attempt to run your program again. If you are using a preprocessor as part of your COBOL system, you should use the software as a standalone preprocessor to isolate the problem areas.

RT203   CALL parameter not supplied

Severity: Fatal

Explanation: You have not supplied your currently
                    executing program with all of the parameters
                    mentioned in the linkage section of your main
                    program.

Resolution: Recode your program to ensure that it
                    contains all of the necessary parameters, or
                    check that it is a valid caller.

RT206   Reading unwritten data from memory file

Severity: Fatal

Explanation: You are attempting to read data which has
                    not been written, from the core file.

RT207   Machine does not exist

Severity: Recoverable

Explanation: You have tried to access a machine that is not
                    connected to your network, or if the machine
                    is part of your network, it is not online.

Resolution: Make sure the machine is connected to the
                    network and online, then attempt to access it
                    again.

RT208   Error in multi-user system

Severity: Recoverable

Explanation: This is normally caused by an unexpected
                    error occurring within the network or file-
                    sharing facilities. A corrupted network
                    message will also return this error.

Error Messages

Resolution: You may be able to recover from this error by executing a COMMIT statement.

RT209   Network communication error

Severity: Recoverable

Explanation: This is normally given if an incorrect checksum has been received in a communications packet.

Resolution: Your program should continue to execute after you have received this error but the effect of the error is undefined.

RT210   File is closed with lock

Severity: Fatal

Explanation: You have tried to open a file which you have previously closed with lock.

Resolution: Recode your program to avoid opening a file which has previously been closed with lock.

RT211   Program linked with wrong library

Severity: Fatal

Explanation: You have tried to link a program that is incompatible with the current version of either your Run-Time System, your object file or your COBOL run-time library. For example, your Run-Time System will not run a program linked using a different object file format or COBOL run-time library.

Resolution: If your object file is incompatible with the current version of either your COBOL run-time library or your Run-Time System, you will need to resubmit your object file to your COBOL system, and then relink with the current version of your COBOL run-time library. Otherwise, you will just need to relink your program.

RT212   Malformed assembler subroutine file

Severity: Fatal

Explanation: You are attempting to access an assembler routine that is not in the specific format for such a file.

Resolution: Examine the example assembler routine which was supplied to you with your system and alter the structure of your routine to be the same as this. Ensure that it is linked properly, it has the correct structure, and you used the right assembler. You should then be able to run your code successfully.

RT213   Too many locks

Severity: Recoverable

Explanation: You have either tried to exceed the maximum number of simultaneous record locks per file you can have, or you have exhausted an operating system or network resource, for example dynamic memory.

Resolution: Execute a COMMIT or an UNLOCK operation on the relevant file and you should then be able to continue to run your program. You should not try to retain a record lock for longer than it is necessary, and this should help to prevent the occurrence of this error.

Error Messages

RT214   GO TO has not been ALTERed

Severity: Fatal

Explanation: You have violated one of the general rules of
                           COBOL programming.

Resolution: CLOSE any files which may be OPEN,
                           execute a STOP RUN statement and then edit
                           your program to avoid such illegal
                           operations.

RT218   Malformed MULTIPLE REEL/UNIT file

Severity: Fatal

Explanation: Your file header is not correctly formatted, or
                           you are not using a MULTIPLE REEL/UNIT
                           file.

Resolution: You will have to attempt to run your program
                           again using a backup copy of the relevant file.

RT219   Operating system shared file limit
             exceeded

Severity: Recoverable

Explanation: You have tried to exceed your operating
                           system's limit on the number of shared files
                           that you can have OPEN simultaneously. As
                           this figure is operating system dependent,
                           you will need to consult your Release Notes
                           for details of how many shared files your
                           system permits to be OPEN at any one time.

Resolution: CLOSE some of the open shared files you are
                           no longer accessing and retry the file
                           operation.

RT220   Attempt to execute more than one SORT or MERGE simultaneously

Severity: Fatal

Explanation: You have coded your program in such a way
                     that it is attempting to execute more than one
                     SORT or MERGE operation at the same time.
                     For example, you may have coded a SORT
                     statement in the input or output procedure of
                     another SORT statement, an operation that is
                     specifically prohibited under the rules of
                     ANSI COBOL.

Resolution: You will have to recode your program to
                     ensure that it does not execute more than one
                     SORT at any one time.

RT221   SORT/MERGE error: see status key

Severity: Fatal

Explanation: You receive one of these three errors if you
                     attempt a SORT/MERGE operation which is
                     unsuccessful for some reason. These errors
                     can result from a variety of causes; for
                     example, you may have too many files OPEN
                     when you attempt a SORT/MERGE
                     operation, or the file which you are trying to
                     access may be locked.

Resolution: The action you should take if you receive one
                     of these errors depends on the situation in
                     which it occurs.

RT222   SORT/MERGE error: see status key

Severity: Fatal

Explanation: You receive one of these three errors if you
                     attempt a SORT/MEGE operation which is
                     unsuccessful for some reason. These errors
                     can result from a variety of causes; for

Error Messages

example, you may have too many files OPEN when you attempt a SORT/MERGE operation, or the file which you are trying to access may be locked.

Resolution: The action you should take if you receive one of these errors depends on the situation in which it occurs.

RT223 SORT/MEGE error: see status key

Severity: Fatal

Explanation: You receive one of these three errors if you attempt a SORT/MEGE operation which is unsuccessful for some reason. These errors can result from a variety of causes; for example, you may have too many files OPEN when you attempt a SORT/MERGE operation, or the file which you are trying to access may be locked.

Resolution: The action you should take if you receive one of these errors depends on the situation in which it occurs.

RT225 Program Component not found

Severity: Fatal

Explanation: You are attempting to load a program overlay which is not present in the expected directory. Alternatively, a program component which was previously located can no longer be found because it has been deleted or the application has changed to a different directory.

Resolution: Ensure that the program files are always readily available.

RT226   EXTERNAL file definition inconsistent

Severity: Fatal

Explanation: The definition of an EXTERNAL file contained in the program being loaded is inconsistent with its definition in a previously loaded program.

RT254   Keyboard interrupt to ANIMATOR during ACCEPT

Severity: Fatal

Explanation: While using ANIMATOR you have terminated your program with a keyboard interrupt.

Error Messages

Index

T

U

V

W

X

Z